The Doctrine of Salvation

The Doctrine of Salvation

By
Charles M. Horne

MOODY PRESS
CHICAGO

ISBN 0-8024-0424-3

1   2   3   4   5   6   7 Printing/ BC /Year 88   87   86   85   84

Printed in the United States of America

Contents

Foreword

It is with a prayer of gratitude that I greet the re-publication of the late Charles Horne's extremely useful handbook on soteriology. I studied soteriology (the doctrine of salvation) under Dr. Horne in 1971) and used this book as a classroom text and guide. It is therefore with deep appreciation that I commend this work to the Christian church.

Here the Christian student will find a basic, nontechnical treatise well suited for personal study, more formal classroom use, or as a Sunday school guide. Dr. Horne has ably distilled the essence of the great evangelical and Reformation teaching on salvation. He sees its complexity, in that the doctrine of salvation embraces many biblical concepts such as election, calling, regeneration, and conversion. But he is able also to see its unity and harmony in pointing us again and again to the grace of God as the well-spring of fallen human beings' salvation.

Dr. Horne was a thorough teacher who delighted in showing his students how to think critically and carefully. He never seemed to leave the important stones unturned. His manner was soft-spoken but his commitment to the grace of God in every aspect of man's salvation came from a deeply held conviction. He had come to see, through a series of changes in his own thinking, that salvation does not in any sense begin with man's activity, because man is hopelessly lost and "dead in trespasses and sins." God does more, therefore, than make the salvation of men *possible*—God *saves* sinners! Thus Dr. Horne liked to exhort his classes to return to the classical evangelical theology of the past—to the beliefs of such men as Calvin, Luther, Whitefield, and Spurgeon. His statements were often challenged by his students but Dr. Horne always drove them back to the Word of God as well as to the great men of the past. Therefore, he made his students *struggle* with truth. He believed, with strong feeling, that we ought to "buy the truth and sell it not" (Prov. 23:23). For me, as I am sure for many others, the truths contained in this little book began to stir the mind and heart profoundly.

Perhaps a new printing of this fine book will challenge another decade of Bible students and teachers. Increasingly today many Christians are taking a more serious interest in good Bible doctrine, and it is hoped this work will help such ones to have a better knowledge of the God of our fathers.

Dr. John H. Armstrong, Pastor
Trinity Baptist Church
Wheaton, Illinois

Introduction

The doctrine of salvation is central to the message of Scripture. From Genesis 3 through Revelation 22 we witness the unfolding drama of redemption. No sooner had man fallen than God is seen promising deliverance (Gen. 3:15). In event, word, and type the entire Old Testament is *anticipatory* of the coming of Jesus Christ; and the New Testament is both a record of that event and an authoritative reflection on its meaning. Man's problem, from his fall in Adam down through the ages, has been both a lack of knowledge of God and a sense of guilt before Him. The answer to this twofold difficulty is found only in the redemptive revelation of God's love in Christ, witnessed to in the Bible.

The salvation planned, executed, and applied by the triune God is manifold in nature. It is comprehended in a series of biblical concepts: election, calling, regeneration, conversion, justification, adoption, sanctification, and glorification. No one of these scriptural terms is fully adequate to explain the meaning of salvation. In the ultimate and fullest sense no man is saved until he has been glorified (1 Cor. 5:5).

It is the purpose of this study to provide some guidance in a systematic way through the biblical materials relating to the concept of salvation. Both the organization and the content (but particularly the latter), while representing the confessional position of the author, are intended primarily to provide the basis for the reader's own constructive interaction; with the desire that each one may engage in an unrelenting effort to construct "his own theology"—a theology which is both exegetically responsible and existentially relevant. C. S. Lewis well states, "The glory of God, and, as our only means to glorifying Him, the salvation of human souls, is the real business of life."[1]

Theology is an ongoing work. May we always be willing to test our present ideas by any new insight which may be gained through our continuing study of the Word. Let us never become so enslaved to any particular theological frame of reference that we cannot accommodate further contributions, which others may offer us, to a more adequate understanding of God's revelation.

In accord with this approach, the works suggested for further reading do not always represent the position of the author but are intended to offer the basis for additional stimulating exploration of the concept under consideration. We frequently learn the most from those who differ from us. With proper guidance such reading can promote the cultivation of a constructive critical sense, a much needed tool in the learning process.

May this study outline, then, bring its reader into a greater understanding of God's redeeming grace, and encourage a clearer witness to those yet without hope and God in the world.

---

1. C. S. Lewis, *Christian Reflections* (Grand Rapids: Eerdmans, 1967), 14.

1
The Need for Salvation

A THOROUGH DISCUSSION of the need for salvation would require a separate volume on biblical anthropology; but a failure to outline certain salient features in this area would greatly disadvantage our consideration of the doctrine of salvation (soteriology). Whenever the church proclaims the good news of salvation, modern man asks, Salvation from what, and why?

MAN'S SIN

If these questions are answered in biblical terms the reply is, From sin so that we may live in fellowship with God and those of like faith both here and hereafter.

NATURE OF SIN

We must ask, what is sin? To this question the Westminster Catechism correctly responds, "Sin is any want of conformity to the law of God, or transgression of it" (cf. 1 John 3:4). This definition is consistently biblical as far as it goes but it stops short at a crucial point. Sin, as biblically described, is not only a failure to obey the law of God and/or a violation of it; it is also—and perhaps even more significantly—a deification of self and a dethronement of God. It is the disruption of the creature's personal relationship with his Creator.

1

As the Puritan Ralph Venning writes,

> In short, sin is the dare of God's justice, the rape of his mercy, the jeer of his patience, the slight of his power, the contempt of his love. . . . We may go on and say, it is the upbraiding of his providence (Psalm 50), the scoff of his promise (2 Peter 3:3-4), the reproach of his wisdom (Isaiah 29:16).[1]

TRANSMISSION OF SIN

Adam's sin has been imputed to all by virtue of the fact of the solidarity of the race and the principle of representation (cf. Rom. 5:12 ff.). All sinned representatively in the one and therefore all inherit a sinful nature from which flows every sinful act. The root of man's perversity is the sinful nature inherited because of his fall in Adam; the fruits are the sinful works which he does (Gal. 5:19-21). Man's predicament is the result of his wickedness—inherited and actual.

Man as a Sinner

Brunner, Emil. *Man in Revolt; A Christian Anthropology.* Philadelphia: Westminster, 1947.

Custance, Arthur. *Man in Adam and in Christ.* The Doorway Papers. Vol. 3. Grand Rapids: Zondervan, 1975.

McDonald, H. D. *The Christian View of Man.* Westchester, Ill.: Crossway, 1981.

Murray, John. *The Imputation of Adam's Sin.* Grand Rapids: Eerdmans, 1959.

Shedd, Russell Philip. *Man in Community.* London: Epworth, 1958. Reprint. Grand Rapids: Eerdmans, n.d.

MAN'S PREDICAMENT

The result of sin is estrangement from God, one's fellowman, and even from oneself. Man is a victim of anxiety, frustration, dread, and despair. Life seems ultimately meaningless, absurd, just a rat race; there is no exit from its fixed maze. With "the preacher" (*Qoheleth*) of old, man concludes, "I observed all the deeds done under the sun, and saw that all was an empty breath and a grasping at the wind" (Eccles. 1:14, Anchor Bible).

Signs of man's desperateness continually scream at us from the press, radio, and television. They show up clearly in the lyrics of some rock music groups. If we are to meet today's challenge we must study the forms in which man expresses his interpretation of existence. These

---

1. Ralph Venning, *The Plague of Plagues* (London: Banner of Truth, 1965), 32.

forms would include the scientific, economic, political, ethical, and artistic realms.

Man's Predicament

Anderson, Ray S. *On Being Human: Essays in Theological Anthropology.* Grand Rapids: Eerdmans, 1982.

Evans, C. Stephen. *Existentialism: The Philosophy of Despair and the Quest for Hope.* Grand Rapids: Zondervan, 1984.

Guinness, Os. *Dust of Death.* Downers Grove, Ill.: Inter-Varsity, 1973.

Schaeffer, Francis A. *Escape from Reason.* London: Inter-Varsity, 1968.

———. *The God Who Is There.* London: Hodder and Stoughton, 1968.

Tillich, Paul. *Theology of Culture.* New York: Oxford U., 1959. (See esp. chapter 6, "Protestantism and Artistic Style.")

The Discovery Series. New York: Association.
Discovery in Drama, 1969.
Discovery in Song, 1968.
Discovery in Word, 1968.
Discovery in the Press, 1969.
Discovery in Film, 1969.

Man is by nature totally depraved. This does not mean that every man is as bad as he can possibly be. Rather, it means that the principle of sin has pervaded every aspect of his nature and he is totally incapable of achieving his own salvation.

The functioning of his intellect has become darkened by sin so that he cannot understand the things of the Spirit of God. Paul states, "An unspiritual man does not accept the things that the Spirit of God teaches, for they are nonsense to him, and he cannot understand them, because they are appreciated by spiritual insight" (1 Cor. 2:14, *Williams*).

Paul has been speaking of that revelation given to the apostolic circle in words taught by the Holy Spirit (v. 13). Much of this material now comprises the verbally inspired ("God-breathed") canon of holy Scripture. In verse 14 the apostle next indicates that these things ("the things that the Spirit of God teaches") were not known by the natural, or unspiritual, man. Special revelation, not general, is under consideration in this passage.

By "unspiritual man" Paul means that man who is only worldly-wise, the man bounded by the things of this life, the unregenerate man. Such a man does not *accept* the things of the Spirit. The verb translated "accept" has in it the idea of welcoming, being the usual word for receiving a guest. Thus the thought is that the natural man does not welcome the things of the Spirit; he refuses them, he rejects them. He is without the necessary ability to discern the revelations of God's Spirit.

Paul now states the reasons why the natural man does not welcome the things of God. First, to an unenlightened mind they are "nonsense"—absurd, insipid, powerless. It is interesting to note that our English word *moron* is derived from the Greek term employed here. The things of the Spirit of God are quite literally moronic to the sinner.

Second, it is asserted that the unbeliever *cannot* understand them. The unrenewed man cannot even begin to discern the truth of divine things. It is not simply that he will not; he cannot. When we inquire as to why he cannot, we discover that it is not because of a faulty functioning of the powers of logical reasoning as such but rather because of a failure to reckon with all pertinent data—data made available only by the work of the Holy Spirit.

Other passages which ought to be noted in this regard are: Romans 3:11; 2 Corinthians 10:5; Titus 1:15; Ephesians 5:8; 2 Peter 2:14.

Thomas Boston writes:

> There is a natural weakness in the minds of men, with respect to spiritual things: the apostle determines concerning every one that is not endued with the graces of the Spirit, "That he is blind and cannot see afar off" 2 Pet. 1:9. . . . Many that are eagle-eyed in the trifles of time, are like owls and bats in the light of life. Nay, truly, the life of every natural man is but one continued dream and delusion, out of which he never awakes, till either, by a new light darted from heaven into his soul, he comes to himself (Luke 15:17), or "in hell he lift up his eyes;" (Luke 16:23). Therefore, in Scripture account, be he never so wise, he is a fool, and a simple one.[2]

Third, it is stated that the unbeliever cannot know them because they are spiritually discerned. According to Leon Morris, the verb translated "discern"

> is that used in a legal sense of the preliminary examination prior to the main hearing (the corresponding noun is used of such a preliminary examination in Acts 25:26). It comes to mean "to scrutinize," "to examine," and so "to judge of," "to estimate." It may be that the use of a verb proper to such a preliminary examination is by way of reminding us that all human verdicts are no more than preliminary. It is God who gives the final verdict. Be that as it may, Paul is insisting that the man whose equipment is only of this world, the man who has not received the Holy Spirit of God, has not the ability to make an estimate of things spiritual.[3]

2. Thomas Boston, *Human Nature in Its Fourfold State* (London: Banner of Truth, 1964), 79 ff.
3. Leon Morris, *The First Epistle of Paul to the Corinthians,* Tyndale New Testament Commentaries, ed. R. V. G. Tasker (Grand Rapids: Eerdmans, 1958), 60.

Man's will is bound in servitude to sin. Again Paul states, "The mind set on the flesh is hostile toward God; for it does not subject itself to the Law of God, for it is not even able to do so; and those who are in the flesh cannot please God" (Rom. 8:7-8, NASB*). Regarding this passage Martin Luther wrote, "Now let us see what Paul thinks about endeavour and the power of "freewill" in carnal men. . . . Let the guardian of 'free-will' answer the following question: How can endeavours towards good be made by that which is death, and displeases God, and is enmity against God, and disobeys God, and cannot obey him?"[4]

Calvin comments,

> Paul. . . declares that our heart is so swollen with hardness and unconquerable obstinacy that it is never moved to submit to the yoke of God naturally. He is not arguing about one or other of the affections, but uses an indefinite expression to cover all the emotions which arise within us. Let the Christian heart therefore drive far from itself the non-Christian philosophy of the freedom of the will, and let every one of us acknowledge himself to be, as in reality he is, the servant of sin, that he may be freed by the grace of Christ and set at liberty. It is the height of folly to boast of any other freedom.[5]

We may diagram man's threefold state in respect to the problem of the will as follows:

ORIGINAL STATE	FALLEN STATE	REDEEMED STATE	
		Present Aspect	Future Aspect
Power not to sin but able to sin	Power only to sin	Power not to sin but able to sin	Not able to sin
Freedom of the will	Bondage of the will	Freedom of the will	Freedom of the will
ADAM AND EVE	THOSE IN THE FIRST ADAM	THOSE IN THE LAST ADAM	THOSE IN THE LAST ADAM

---

*New American Standard Bible.

4. Martin Luther, *The Bondage of the Will* (Westwood, N. J.: Revell, 1957), 300.
5. John Calvin, *The Epistles of Paul the Apostle to the Romans and to the Thessalonians,* Calvin's Commentaries, vol. 8, Ross Mackenzie, trans., and D. W. Torrance and T. F. Torrance, eds. (Grand Rapids: Eerdmans, 1961), 163.

There are several things to note regarding fallen man.

1. Fallen man may not do an absolute good.

2. He may, and frequently does, do relative good because of God's common grace.

3. The fallen man's choices fall within the context of a servitude to sin (Rom. 6:17, 20).

4. The only way out of this bondage to sin is God's redeeming grace.

Man's emotions are base, inordinate. The writer of Proverbs speaks of the wicked, for example, "Who delight in doing evil, and exult in evil's perversity" (Prov. 2:14, *New Berkeley*).

Arminius gives a very clear statement of man's state before and after the fall.

> In his primitive condition as he came out of the hands of his Creator, man was endowed with such a portion of knowledge, holiness and power, as enabled him to understand, esteem, consider, will, and to perform THE TRUE GOOD, according to the commandment delivered to him. Yet none of these acts could he do, *except through the assistance of Divine Grace.* But in his *lapsed and sinful state,* man is not capable, of and by himself, either to think, to will, or to do that which is really good; but it is necessary for him to be regenerated and renewed in his intellect, affections or will, and in all his powers, by God in Christ through the Holy Spirit, that he may be qualified rightly to understand, esteem, consider, will, and perform whatever is truly good.[6]

The prophet Jeremiah sums it up well: "The heart [man in the totality of his being] is deceitful above all things, and desperately wicked: who can know it?" (Jer. 17:9, KJV*). In the words of Paul, the natural man is spiritually dead (Eph. 2:1).

Man's Bondage to Sin

Berkouwer, G. C. *Sin.* Grand Rapids: Zondervan, 1971.

Jaspers, Karl. *Man in the Modern Age.* Garden City, N.Y.: Doubleday, Anchor, 1957.

Trueblood, Elton. *The Predicament of Modern Man.* New York: Harper, Chapel, 1944.

Venning, Ralph. *The Plague of Plagues.* London: Banner of Truth, 1965.

---

*King James Version.

6. James Arminius, *The Writings of James Arminius,* vol. 1 (Grand Rapids: Baker, 1956), 252.

2
The Basis of Salvation

WE MUST MAKE a distinction here between the ultimate basis and the instrumental basis of salvation: The former involves God's sovereign electing grace, the latter His sending of His Son to accomplish this elective purpose; the former is a matter of God's eternal purpose, the latter, His execution of that purpose in history.

GOD'S ETERNAL COUNSEL—ELECTION

It is not the purpose of this study to present a comprehensive treatment of the doctrine of election, but rather to present the essence of this biblical concept as seen in its relation to the doctrine of salvation. With this purpose in mind we shall briefly state three main views and then examine two key Scripture passages.

THREE MAJOR VIEWS

ARMINIAN

The *Arminian view* holds that God elects on the basis of foreseen faith. Henry C. Thiessen states the position clearly: "By election we mean that sovereign act of God in grace whereby He chose in Christ Jesus for salvation all those whom He foreknew would accept Him."[1]

---

1. Henry Clarence Thiessen, *Introductory Lectures in Systematic Theology* (Grand Rapids: Eerdmans, 1949), 343.

7

Thiessen develops his argument as follows:

1. Election is a sovereign act of God in that He was under no obligation to elect anyone. All stand equally condemned before God because of sin, and therefore all could have been justly damned.

2. It was an act of grace in that He chose those who were utterly undeserving.

3. It was "in Christ"; He (the Father) chose in the merits of His Son.

4. He chose those whom He foreknew would believe. On this point appeal is made to Romans 8:29-30 and 1 Peter 1:1-2.

5. It is understood that God graciously grants to all men sufficient ability to accept Christ. "This is the salvation—bringing the grace of God that has appeared to all men. In His foreknowledge He perceives what each one will do with this restored ability, and elects men to salvation in harmony with His knowledge of their choice of Him."[2]

Arminian View of Election

Arminius, James. *The Writings of James Arminius.* Vol. 1. Grand Rapids: Baker, 1956. Pages 380-81.

Carter, Charles W., ed. *A Contemporary Wesleyan Theology.* 2 vols. Grand Rapids: Zondervan, 1983.

Foster, Roger T., and V. Paul Marston. *God's Strategy in Human History.* Wheaton, Ill.: Tyndale, 1974.

BARTHIAN

According to the *Barthian view,* election is, primarily, the election of Jesus Christ; secondly, the election of the community; and, thirdly, the election of the individual. The first of these is most important for Barth's doctrine. The doctrine of reconciliation in Christ can be understood only in terms of the mystery of God's decisive word of election in Christ. Election in Christ is the miracle which God has worked among *all* men. This wonderful miracle is that Jesus Christ is *at the same time* the electing God and the elect man. While it is necessary to speak of a double predestination, this may be done only in terms of Golgatha. This elect man is also the rejected man, the one who endures the wrath of God to the end. There is no question here of a distribution of election and reprobation over such and such people but only of double predestination in and concerning Christ. Barth states, "In its simplest and most comprehensive form the dogma of predestination consists, then, in the assertion that the divine predestination is the election of Jesus

2. Ibid., 344.

Christ . . . Jesus Christ is the electing God, and . . . also elected man."[3]

Barth's radical revision of the Reformation view of election inevitably raises the question of whether his view does not require as a logical corollary the acceptance of a consistent universalism. Barth replies No! Berkouwer writes, however, "There is no alternative to concluding that Barth's refusal to accept the *apokatastasis* [universalism] cannot be harmonized with the fundamental structure of his doctrine of election."[4]

Henry Buis writes, "Since Barth says that all men are elect in Christ, that the basic difference between believers and unbelievers is only that the unbeliever doesn't know as yet that he is elected and that because Jesus took upon himself the rejection of man, no man is rejected, it is difficult to see how Barth can stop short of universalism."[5]

Barth's view of election makes evangelization an announcement of the sinner's acceptance in Christ rather than an invitation for him to repent; thus, in his sermons to prisoners he begins, "Dear brothers and sisters."

Barthian View of Election

Barth, Karl. *Church Dogmatics*. Vol. 2,2. New York: Scribner's, 1957.
Berkouwer, Gerrit C. *The Triumph of Grace in the Theology of Karl Barth*. Grand Rapids: Eerdmans, 1956.
Criterion, (Winter 1963), p. 11.
Maury, Pierre. *Predestination, and other Papers*. Richmond: Knox, 1960.
Torrance, T. F. "Predestination in Christ." *Evangelical Quarterly* 13 (1941): 108-31.

CALVINIST

The *Calvinistic view* states that God elects unconditionally; there is nothing in the creature which conditions His choice of some and passing over of others. Berkhof states the position clearly: Election is "that eternal act of God whereby He, in His sovereign good pleasure, and on account of no foreseen merit in them, chooses a certain number of men

---

3. Karl Barth, *Church Dogmatics* (Edinburgh: T & T Clark, 1959, vol. 2: part 2, 103.
4. G. C. Berkouwer, *The Triumph of Grace in the Theology of Karl Barth* (Grand Rapids: Eerdmans, 1956), 116. Emil Brunner concurs in this judgment (*Christian Doctrine of God*, Dogmatics, vol. 1 [Philadelphia: Westminster, 1950], 346-53).
5. Harry Buis, *Historic Protestantism and Predestination* (Philadelphia: Presb. & Ref., 1958), 103.

to be the recipients of special grace and of eternal salvation."[6] Berkhof outlines the characteristics of election as follows:

1. It finds its moving cause in the sovereign will of God, His divine good pleasure.

2. It renders certain the salvation of those chosen in Christ (Rom. 8:29-30).

3. It is from eternity and is not to be confused with the idea of *temporal* selection (Eph. 1:4-5).

4. It is unconditional; it does not in any way depend upon the foreseen faith or good works of man. It rests exclusively upon the sovereign good pleasure of God who is also the giver of faith (Acts 13:48; Rom. 9:11; 2 Tim. 1:9; 1 Pet. 1:2).

5. It is irresistible. "This does not mean that man cannot oppose its execution to a certain degree, but it does mean that his opposition will not prevail. Neither does it mean that God in the execution of His decree overpowers the human will in a manner which is inconsistent with man's free agency. It does mean, however, that God can and does exert such an influence on the human spirit as to make it willing. Ps. 110:3; Phil. 2:13."[7]

Calvinistic View of Election

Berkouwer, G. C. *Divine Election*. Grand Rapids: Eerdmans, 1960.

Boettner, Loraine. *The Reformed Doctrine of Predestination*. Philadelphia: Presbyterian and Reformed, 1965.

Calvin, John. *Institutes of the Christian Religion*. 3:21-25. Philadelphia: Westminster, n.d.

Daane, James. *The Freedom of God: A Study of Election and the Pulpit*. Grand Rapids: Eerdmans, 1973.

Johns, Kenneth. *Election: Love Before Time*. Philadelphia: Presbyterian and Reformed, 1976.

Shedd, W. G. T. *Dogmatic Theology*. Vol. 1. Grand Rapids: Zondervan, n.d. Pages 422 ff.

TWO KEY SCRIPTURE PASSAGES

EPHESIANS 1:4-5

> He chose us in Him before the foundation of the world, that we should be holy and blameless before Him. In love He predestined us to adoption as sons through Jesus Christ to Himself, according to the kind intention of His will. (Eph. 1:4-5, NASB)

---

6. L. Berkhof, *Systematic Theology* (Grand Rapids: Eerdmans, 1941), 114.
7. Ibid., 114-15.

This passage teaches us a number of important ideas.

1. The source of our election: "He [the Father] chose us."

2. The sphere of our election: "He [the Father] chose us in Him [Christ]." Reformation theology maintains that there is a decision of God which precedes this election in Christ; as we noted previously, Barth denies such. He maintains that we may not think of an independent decree of God as standing behind the revelation in Jesus Christ, but that in the most literal sense of the word we must view election exclusively in Jesus Christ. He is the electing God and the elected one.

3. The time of our election: "Before the foundation of the world." We have been the objects of God's eternal choice.

4. The purposes of our election: "That we should be holy and blameless." If Paul's reference here is to sanctification then we may conclude two things. First, holiness cannot be the ground of election. If men are chosen to be holy they cannot be chosen because they are holy. Second, holiness is the evidence of election. It is a contradiction in terms for one to claim to be elected unto holiness and to live in sin.

Another purpose of our election is adoption: "In love He predestined us to adoption as sons." The doctrine of adoption will be discussed later.

Also, God has foreordained us "to Himself." God's ultimate object in so predestinating us is His own glory.

5. The motive behind our election: "In love He predestined us." (There is some question of just how "love" is to be construed here, but the rendering of the NASB and RSV* seems preferable to that of the KJV.)

6. The basis of our election—"According to the kind intention of His will." Paul seems to teach here unconditional election. By unconditional it is meant that election is not conditioned by anything in the creature, nor does it in any way depend on anything in the creature whether foreseen faith or good works. It depends entirely on the sovereign good pleasure of God.

Commentaries on Ephesians

Bruce, F. F. *The Epistle to the Ephesians.* Westwood, N. J.: Revell, 1961.

Hendricksen, William. *Exposition of Ephesians.* Grand Rapids: Baker, 1967.

Hodge, Charles. *A Commentary on the Epistle to the Ephesians.* Grand Rapids: Eerdmans, 1950.

Revised Standard Version.

ROMANS 8:28-30

> We know that God causes all things to work together for good to those who love God, to those who are called according to His purpose. For whom He foreknew, He also predestined to become conformed to the image of His son, that He might be the first-born among many brethren; and whom He predestined, these He also called; and whom He called, these He also justified; and whom He justified, these He also glorified. (Rom. 8:28-30, NASB)

This passage is most important in establishing the link between God's eternal purpose and the execution of that purpose—soteriologically conceived. The renowned Lutheran scholar Anders Nygren has expressed this connection well.

> These are mighty affirmations which are closely knit together and stretch *from eternity—through time—to eternity*. The concept of the two aeons is here transcended. *Before* the old aeon stands God's eternal purpose. "Before the foundation of the world" God fixed His purpose of election. It is that which now moves on toward realization in the world, when God calls and justifies men. And it is that which He will bring to consummation in eternity, when He glorifes themn. Paul would thus show how everything—from the eternal election to the final glory—is utterly in God's hand. There is place for neither chance nor arbitrariness.[8]

God's eternal counsel involves foreknowledge and predestination.

"Whom He foreknew"—the problem here is to ascertain the precise meaning of God's foreknowledge. Sometimes the word translated "foreknew" is used in the sense of "to know beforehand" (cf. Acts 26:5; 2 Pet. 3:17). It could therefore refer to God's eternal prevision, His foresight of all that would come to pass. Some expositors, such as H. P. Liddon,[9] have argued for such a meaning here.

If the meaning here is simply "to know beforehand" then we naturally ask, By what distinguishing element have those referred to in our text been differentiated? Clearly Paul does not give us the answer to this question here. Various answers have been proposed; among the most common is that what is in view is God's foresight of faith.

Now even if we granted that *foreknew* means foresight of faith (and we cannot, for reasons to be stated below), the biblical doctrine of unconditional election is not thereby refuted. We would simply be forced to ask another question: Whence this faith which God foresees? And the only *biblical* answer that we can discover is that the faith which God

---

8. Anders Nygren, *Commentary on Romans* (Philadelphia: Muhlenburg, 1949), 340.
9. H. P. Liddon, *Explanatory Analysis of St. Paul's Epistle to the Romans* (Grand Rapids: Zondervan, 1961), 139.

foresees He sovereignly bestows. (Cf. John 3:3-8; 6:44-45, 65; Eph. 2:8; 1 Pet. 1:2). As Professor John Murray has stated, "Hence his eternal foresight of faith is pre-conditioned by his decree to generate this faith in those whom he foresees as believing, and we are thrown back upon the differentiation which proceeds from God's own eternal and sovereign election to faith and its consequences."[10]

But—and this is important—the text states, "Whom he foreknew." *Whom* is the object of the verb and there is no qualifying addition. This fact of itself would suggest that the expression "whom he foreknew" contains within itself the distinguishing element which is presupposed. "If the apostle had in mind some 'qualifying adjunct' 'it would have been simple to supply it. Since he adds none we are forced to inquire if the actual terms he uses can express the differentiation implied. The usage of Scripture provides an affirmative answer."[11] The following Scriptures establish clearly that many times the word *know* has a meaning which goes beyond mere cognition, suggesting the pregnant idea of "love," "to set regard upon," "to know with peculiar interest," "delight," "affection": Genesis 18:19; Exodus 2:25; Psalm 1:6; 144:3; Jeremiah 1:5; Hosea 13:5; Amos 3:2; Matthew 7:23; 1 Corinthians 8:3; Galatians 4:9; 2 Timothy 2:19; 1 John 3:1.

Predestination in Pauline Theology

Davidson, Francis. *Pauline Predestination*. London: Tyndale, 1945.
Moffat, James. *Predestination*. New York: Loizeaux, n.d.

Thus by way of conclusion, "whom He foreknew" may best be taken to mean "whom He set regard upon" or "whom He knew from eternity with distinguishing affection and delight" and is virtually equivalent to "whom He foreloved."

"He also predestined"—those upon whom God set His sovereign distinguishing love He has determined ("predestined") to be conformed to the image of His Son. *Foreknew* focuses attention on the basis for our election; *predestined*, the destination to which those thus chosen are appointed.

The two preceding verses (Romans 8:28-29) deal with the eternal counsel of God, explaining it in terms of foreknowledge and predestination. The apostle now turns his attention (v. 30) to the temporal

---

10. John Murray, *The Epistle to the Romans,* New International Commentary on the New Testament, vol. 1, ed. Ned B. Stonehouse (Grand Rapids: Eerdmans, 1959), 316.
11. Ibid., 317.

realization, the actualization, of that purpose in the children of God. This he does in terms of three divine actions—calling, justification, and glorification—which we simply mention here because of fuller treatment later.

The structure of this passage may be diagramatically represented as follows:

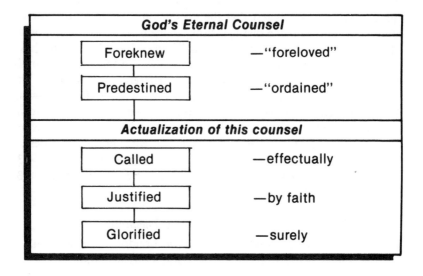

God's Eternal Counsel	
Foreknew	—"foreloved"
Predestined	—"ordained"
Actualization of this counsel	
Called	—effectually
Justified	—by faith
Glorified	—surely

("Glorified" is in the past tense, thus indicating the certainty of the event. This last link in the unbreakable chain of God's redemptive work is here viewed from the divine perspective as an accomplished fact.)

Commentaries on Romans

Bruce, F. F. *The Epistle of Paul to the Romans.* The Tyndale New Testament Commentaries. Grand Rapids: Eerdmans, 1963.

Harrison, Everett F. "Romans." In *The Expositor's Bible Commentary,* vol. 10, edited by Frank E. Gaebelein. Grand Rapids: Zondervan, 1976.

Hodge, Charles. *Commentary on the Epistle to the Romans.* Grand Rapids: Eerdmans, 1950.

Johnson, Alan F. *The Freedom Letter.* Chicago: Moody, 1974.

CHRIST'S REDEMPTIVE WORK—HISTORY

What God determined in His eternal counsel He accomplished in history. "God carries out his plan in connection with specific temporal events."[12] This is an area of major dispute in present theological controversy.[13] Two major views may be noted.

EXISTENTIAL SCHOOL

According to Bultmann, the essence of the Christian message is *a call to decision,* which gives the basis of a new understanding of oneself. Bultmann almost entirely divorces the question of existence in the New Testament from that of salvation history. Cullmann significantly observes that "the demand to align one's self with a coherent, special, divine history comprehending past, present, and future is a conception of salvation far removed from, and alien to, modern thinking."[14]

Carl F. H. Henry states,

> The long failure of German theology to reject the existential-dialectical notion that the historical aspects of the Christian revelation are dispensable gave to Continental dogmatics something of the atmosphere of an exclusive private club. Membership was restricted mainly to scholars who shared the speculative dogma that spiritual truth cannot be unified with historical and scientific truth. They therefore emphasized the kerygmatic Christ at the expense of the Jesus of history, isolated Christianity from answerability to scientific and historical inquiry, and detached theology from philosophic truth.[15]

HISTORICAL SCHOOL

According to Cullmann the essence of the Christian message is both salvation history (*heilsgeschichte*) and Christian existence. "We find that not only call and decision, but also salvation history occupies an essential place in the books of the New Testament."[16] One of the major

---

12. Oscar Cullmann, *Salvation in History* (New York: Harper & Row, 1967), 76.
13. See Carl F. H. Henry, *Frontiers in Modern Theology* (Chicago: Moody, 1966), 41 ff.
14. Cullmann, 21. For an excellent refutation of Bultmann's historical skepticism see Carl E. Braaten, *History and Hermeneutics,* New Discoveries in Theology, vol. 2 (Philadelphia: Westminster, 1966). See also Carl F. H. Henry, "Justification by Ignorance: A Neo-Protestant Motif?" *Christianity Today* (2 Jan. 1970), 10-15.
15. Henry, *Frontiers,* 41.
16. Cullmann, 21.

modalities of special revelation is that of historical event.[17]

One further word should be given to clearly differentiate between the *Heilsgeschichte* scholars and the traditional conservative scholars.

While both schools would agree as to the historical objectivity and divine meaning of God's redemptive work, they would not agree as to the basis on which these biblical events are to be ascertained. The *Heilsgeschichte* school would look to some suprarational existential experience to discern it, whereas the conservative school would look to the divinely inspired record of Scripture.

17. See Bernard Ramm, *Special Revelation and the Word of God* (Grand Rapids: Eerdmans, 1961), 70 ff.

3

The Nature of Salvation

THE NATURE OF SALVATION is seen in a study of the atonement accomplished by God through His Son, Jesus Christ.

NECESSITY OF THE ATONEMENT

There are two principal views that may be observed. The *hypothetical necessity view* maintains that God could have saved His elect without atonement (other means were open to an all-powerful God) but that He chose this means as the best for the accomplishment of His purpose. Two notable exponents of this view were Augustine and Aquinas.[1]

In the *consequent absolute necessity view,* the word *consequent* points to the idea that God did not have to save anyone; but, consequent upon the fact that He determined to do so, this view maintains that He *must* do so by atonement. Among those holding this view were George Smeaton, A. A. Hodge, and L. Berkhof.[2]

This latter view would seem preferable to the former one on the basis

---

1. Cf. Augustine, *On the Trinity,* bk. 13, chap. 10; Aquinas, *Summa Theologica,* pt. 3, q. 46, arts. 2 and 3.
2. Cf. George Smeaton, *The Doctrine of the Atonement as Taught by Christ Himself* (Grand Rapids: Zondervan, 1953), 22 ff.; A. A. Hodge, *The Atonement* (Grand Rapids: Eerdmans, 1953), 243 ff. L. Berkhof, *Systematic Theology* (Grand Rapids: Eerdmans, 1941), 368 ff.

of the following arguments, which are admittedly largely inferential.

1. God's holiness will not allow Him to simply overlook sin; His justice must be maintained (Ex. 34:6-7; Num. 14:18; Neh. 1:3; and esp. Rom. 3:25-26).

2. The immutability of the divine law, as reflective of God's very nature, made it necessary for Him to demand satisfaction of the sinner (Deut. 27:26).

3. The truthfulness of God requires atonement (Num. 23:19; Rom. 3:4). In the garden God had declared that death would be the penalty of disobedience (Gen. 3:16-17; cf. Ezek. 18:4; Rom. 6:23). The veracity of God demanded that this penalty should be executed on either the offender or a substitute.

4. The inestimable cost of this sacrifice implies the necessity of the atonement. It is scarcely conceivable that God would have done this unnecessarily (Luke 24:26; Gal. 3:21; Heb. 2:10; 9:22-23).

THEORIES OF THE ATONEMENT

RANSOM THEORY—ORIGEN (A.D. 185-254)

The ransom theory has sometimes been called the military theory. Those who held it argued that Satan, as a captor in war, had a right to his captives. The only way of release would be by the payment of a ransom to Satan. This view was held in one form or another by a number of the early church Fathers and has thus been called the patristic theory.

Origen, who was a well-known exponent, wrote, " 'A ransom for many.' To whom was it paid? Certainly not to God; can it then be to the evil one? For he had power over us until the ransom was given to him on our behalf, namely the life of Jesus."[3]

How may we evaluate this view? It would seem best to understand the biblical term *ransom* as a figure of speech indicating that our redemption is costly. We sometimes speak of the price which a mother pays when she brings a child into the world, but it would be absurd to ask to whom she pays the price. Likewise, it is meaningless to ask to whom the ransom is paid that effects our redemption.

SATISFACTION THEORY—ANSELM (A.D. 1033—1109)

The satisfaction view is developed in Anselm's book, *Cur Deus Homo*. He set forth the idea of Christ's voluntary discharge of man's obligation to God. He maintained that Christ's death provided full

---

3. Origen, "Commentary on Matthew," 16:8; cf. Henry Bettenson, ed., *The Early Christian Fathers* (London: Oxford U., 1956).

satisfaction for our sins and that His merit was more than equal to any obligation which man could possibly incur toward God.

Anselm argued that "it is . . . not proper for God thus to pass over sin unpunished . . . if sin be passed by unpunished, viz., that with God there will be no difference between the guilty and the not guilty; and this is unbecoming to God . . . Therefore the honor taken away must be repaid, or punishment must follow; otherwise, either God will not be just to himself, or he will be weak in respect to both parties; and this it is impious even to think of."[4]

On the positive side it should be noted that Anselm (1) "performed a splendid service for theology by bringing the doctrine of the atonement out into the forefront of theological consideration"[5]; (2) "he freed the doctrine of the atonement from the grotesque forms of thought in which the patristic doctrine had come to be formulated"[6]; and (3) he took the problem of sin seriously.

On the negative side it should be noted that (1) the theological method employed was totally rationalistic—reason was used apart from the revelation of God in Christ; (2) his system was presented therefore in much too judicial a fashion—his theory "rests upon a view of God in which God, in his supreme concern for his own outraged honor, bears more resemblance to a feudal lord of the Middle Ages than to the God and Father of our Lord Jesus Christ"[7]; (3) his stress upon the concept of satisfaction makes the New Testament concept of God's love recede into the background; and (4) he failed to make it clear that the sinner may only appropriate the benefits of Christ's death through faith.

Otto Heick appropriately summarizes, "Anselm, in this endeavor to systematize the doctrine of the atonement, recognized the fundamental truths of Scripture and of Christian experience involved in man's sin, namely, God's justice and the means of redemption. Despite his imperfect expression, Anselm drew lines that have served as a foundation for arriving at more evangelical forms of teaching."[8]

---

4. S. N. Deane, trans., *Saint Anselm Basic Writings* (LaSalle, Ill.: Open Court Pub., 1962), 203 ff.
5. Robert H. Culpepper, *Interpreting the Atonement* (Grand Rapids: Eerdmans, 1966), 85.
6. Ibid.
7. Ibid., 87.
8. Otto W. Heick, *A History of Christian Thought* (Philadelphia: Fortress, 1965), 1:276.

MORAL INFLUENCE THEORY—ABELARD (A.D. 1079—1142)

The moral influence view is perhaps best understood as a reaction to Anselm's position. As we have noted, Anselm argued for the necessity of the atonement largely on the basis of sheer logic, apart from the historical revelation of God in the Son. He had failed to expound on the love of God which prompted it and the love which it elicits from men. Abelard, on endeavoring to correct Anselm's deficiency, rejected the primary thesis of satisfaction upon which the latter built his view.

The best sources for learning of Abelard's position are his *Epitome of Christian Theology* and his *Commentary on Romans*. In the latter he attacked both the patristic view of a ransom paid to the devil and Anselm's view of satisfaction paid to God. In summary Abelard's own view is that "Christ's birth, passion, and death reveal God's infinite love for mankind and awaken in us a reciprocal love and gratitude. This disposition of love is the basis both of justification and the forgiveness of sin."[9]

Abelard was correct in affirming that the life and death of Christ are the supreme revelation of God's love. In emphasizing this, Abelard corrected what was a glaring weakness of Anselm's view; but Abelard's view is weak in the very place where it is strong. The Scriptures portray the death of Christ as a demonstration of love to *sinners;* that is, His death had some necessary relation to man's sin.

> In denying any objective element in the atonement and by ignoring the great body of scriptural teaching concerning Christ as the ransom for our sins and concerning his bearing our sins, the moral influence view inverts the order. According to Abelard, God saves us by revealing his love. But it is at this point that the moral influence view is most ambiguous. It fails to give an adequate explanation of how the death of Christ is a demonstration of God's love, because it fails to recognize the atonement as an objective act of God through which the sin of man is annulled. The subjective-appropriation of the atonement depends upon the objective fact of the-atonement.[10]

EXAMPLE THEORY—SOCINUS (1539—1604)

The best sources for learning of the Socinian doctrine of the atonement are Faustus Socinus' *De Jesus Christo Servatore* (1549) and the *Racovian Catechism* (1605). Socinus argues that it is inconsistent to combine the grace of God and the merits of Christ as the ground of for-

---

9. Ibid., 277.
10. Culpepper, 91.

giveness; it must be one or the other. Socinus chose the former, namely, that God forgives freely. He also maintained that, since guilt is personal, substitution in penal matters is impossible. Christ's death effected reconciliation by affording motives and encouragements to man to repent and turn to Him. Christ's power to save is based on the truth of His teaching and the influence of His example. The death of Christ is but that of a noble martyr. The modern advocates of this view are the Unitarians.

This view is made up of several heresies condemned by the early church. It is based on a revival of Pelagianism with its belief in the inherent goodness and spiritual ability of man, on the moral influence theory of the atonement with its emphasis on the exemplary life of Christ, on the Scotist doctrine of an arbitrary will in God, and on the old adoptionist doctrine, making Christ as to His human nature a Son of God by adoption.

> If Socinus had been as proficient in stating a constructive view of the atonement as he was in assailing the prevailing view, his contribution to Christian theology would have been tremendous indeed. Unfortunately, however, the untenability of his general theological position made it impossible for him to make such a constructive contribution. There is, of course, truth in the view that Christ in his obedience even unto death is an example for others to follow (I Pet. 2:21-23; Matt. 16:24). However, this is far from being an adequate explanation of the atonement.[11]

GOVERNMENTAL THEORY—GROTIUS (1583—1645)

The Socinian attack on Calvinistic orthodoxy provoked a counterattack, strangely enough from the Arminian Hugo Grotius. This view, set forth in the book *Defense of the Catholic Faith on the Satisfaction of Christ against Faustus Socinus,* maintains that

> the atonement is a satisfaction, not to any internal principle of the divine nature, but to the necessities of government. God's government of the universe cannot be maintained, nor can the divine law preserve its authority over its subjects, unless the pardon of offenders is accompanied by some exhibition of the high estimate which God sets upon his law, and the heinous guilt of violating it. Such an exhibition of divine regard for the law is furnished in the suffering and death of Christ. Christ does not suffer the precise penalty of the law, but God graciously accepts his suffering as a substitute for the penalty.[12]

---

11. Ibid., 105.
12. A. H. Strong, *Systematic Theology* (Chicago: Judson, 1907), 740.

The concern of this theory is not the satisfying of divine justice but its manifestation.

The great strength of Grotius' view is that God is viewed as a moral governor who always acts in the best interests of His subjects. The basic weaknesses are that it uses traditional terminology with nontraditional meaning, and that it fails to explain how God can be both just and the justifier of sinners. It would seem that God works in the atonement on the basis of what is expedient rather than on what is just. "This has sometimes led theologians to caricature Grotius' view by describing it in terms of Caiaphas' statement that it is expedient that one man should die for the people and that the whole nation should not perish (John 11:50)."[13]

DRAMATIC THEORY—GUSTAF AULÉN (1879—1978)

Gustaf Aulén in his book *Christus Victor* claims that the "dramatic" theory of the atonement properly views the essence of Christ's work in terms of man's liberation from the tyrants of sin, law, death, wrath, and the devil. According to Aulén this was the view of the early Fathers, subsequently lost by Anselm and medieval scholasticism but recaptured by Martin Luther. "This classic motif of reconciliation is concerned with drama, warfare, and victory."[14]

By way of evaluation we should note here the comments of Paul Althaus:

> Aulén's interpretation of Luther is not substantiated by the sources. The assertion that Luther provides the basis for Aulén's own dogmatic acceptance of the "classical" type is not true. Luther places the emphasis elsewhere . . . Luther in discussing Christ's work, places primary emphasis on its relationship to God's wrath and thus to our guilt rather than on its relationship to the demonic powers. The satisfaction which God's righteousness demands constitutes the primary and decisive significance of Christ's work and particularly of his death. Everything else depends on this satisfaction, including the destruction of the might and the authority of the demonic powers.[15]

It is true that Scripture speaks in many contexts of Christ's warfare and victory, both in prophecy and in fulfillment. (See John 16:33; cf.

---

13. Culpepper, 108.
14. G. C. Berkouwer, *The Work of Christ, Studies in Dogmatics,* vol. 9 (Grand Rapids: Eerdmans, 1965), 329.
15. Paul Althaus, *The Theology of Martin Luther* (Philadelphia: Fortress, 1966), 220. See also Culpepper, 93 ff.

14:30; Acts 2:23; 2 Cor. 2:14; Col. 2:15; Heb. 2:14; 1 John 3:8; Rev. 5:5; 17:14.)

> The objection to this classical motif is not that it sees and preaches Christ as Warrior and Conqueror. . . . The battle-and-victory motif is both Pauline and Johannine, and calls our attention to the profoundest depth of Christ's work which is apparent already in his humiliation, which depth cannot be understood without seeing it as part of Christ's struggle and victory. . . .
> But it is very necessary to observe that the concept of the nature of the "conquered powers" has frequently changed in the course of history. It has become increasingly more evident that we may not think that we have presented the *kerygma* faithfully when we call Christ Victor and speak of his tremendously powerful battle. For the question is *which* powers Christ Jesus has conquered, and how this victory is seen in the total context of the scriptural testimony. Even after having rediscovered the cosmic perspectives of the gospel, we must formulate our views on the basis of the entire gospel. Precisely while rejecting one-sided views, we must be on our guard against other one-sided views.[16]

PENAL SUBSTITUTIONARY THEORY—CALVIN (1509—1564)

The position of Calvin is presented with great clarity in Book II of his *Institutes of the Christian Religion*. In this work he indicates that since man fell into sin by disobedience, Christ by obedience in the sinner's stead has paid the penalty which we had incurred. "Calvin interprets the death of Christ both in terms of the forensic category of penal substitution and the sacrifical category of a sacrifice for sins which renders God propitious toward us."[17]

Calvin stated, "Our Lord came forth as true man and took the person and the name of Adam in order to take Adam's place in obeying the Father, to present our flesh as the price of satisfaction to God's righteous judgment, and, in the same flesh, to pay the penalty that we had deserved."[18]

Most of the previous views surveyed have elements of truth; but—with the exception of this last one—they may be judged to be inadequate in varying degrees. Christ by His death did make full satisfaction for our sins; He did by His death seek to elicit the love and gratitude of the believer toward Himself and others, but not as a basis of acceptance before God. He did provide an example for believers to

---

16. Berkouwer, 338.
17. Culpepper, 98.
18. John Calvin, *Institutes of the Christian Religion*, Library of Christian Classics, vol. 20, ed. John T. McNeill and Henry P. Van Deusen (Philadelphia: Westminster, 1960), 466.

follow, by His obedience even unto death (1 Pet. 2:21-23; Matt. 16:24). But these are far from adequate explanations of the atonement.

Concerning the Socinian position Berkouwer states,

> The controversy with the Socinians has been one of the most serious in the history of the Church, for it concerns the heart of the Church's teaching regarding the sacrifice of Christ. Those who protest against substitution in the sacrifice of Christ express the natural, inevitable rejection by the human heart; refusing the gift of God, they are left in the poverty of their debt. God's graciousness and justice are revealed only in the real substitution, in the radical sacrifice, in the reversing of roles.[19]

Penal substitution is central to the biblical teaching of atonement. In Isaiah 53:5-6 we read, "He was pierced for our transgressions; He was bruised for our iniquities; the punishment which procured our peace fell upon Him, and with His stripes we are healed . . . and the LORD had laid on Him the iniquity of us all" (*New Berkeley*).

> Whether men will have it or not, this verse (vs. 5) and the one preceding teach very clearly the doctrine of a substitutionary atonement. One cannot read these words without being impressed by the stress that the prophet places upon this thought. So prominent is the idea that one scholar, who was by no means a conservative, felt compelled to write: "Substitutionary suffering is expressed in this Divine oracle in not less than five sentences. It is as though God could not do enough to make this clear."[20]

In the spirit of the prophetic passage cited above, Jesus declared concerning Himself, "The Son of man also came not to be ministered unto but to minister, and to give his life a ransom for many" (Mark 10:45, ASV*). Both the term *ransom (lutron)* and the preposition *for (anti)* indicate substitution. A distinction has frequently been made between "in our behalf" *(huper)* (2 Cor. 5:15; cf. Rom. 5:6, 8; 1 Cor. 15:3) and "in our stead" *(anti)* (Matt. 20:28; Mark 10:45), but it must be noted that many hold that there is no warrant for such a distinction.

> When Christ gives his life a ransom *(lytron),* then life becomes free because He gives his life. "In their favor it is precisely the case that he takes their place" [G. Kittel, *Theologisches Wörterbuch Zum Neuen Testament,* p. 373, s.v. *anti*]. This correctly says that "in the stead of" and "in behalf

---

*American Standard Version.

19. Berkouwer, 311.
20. E. J. Young, *Isaiah Fifty-three: A Devotional and Expository Study* (Grand Rapids: Eerdmans, 1952), 53.

SUMMARY OF MAJOR THEORIES OF THE ATONEMENT

THEORY	ORIGINAL EXPONENT	WRITTEN SOURCE	MAIN IDEA	MORE RECENT EXPONENTS
Ransom	Origen	*Commentary on Matthew*	Ransom paid to the devil	
Satisfaction	Anselm	*Cur Deus Homo?*	Satisfaction rendered to God's justice	Schleiermacher Ritschl Bushnell
Moral Influence	Abelard	*Commentary on Romans*	An answering love securing redemption	
Example	Socinus	*De Jesu Christo Servatore*	An imitation of Christ's teaching and example bringing redemption	Altizer
Governmental	Grotius	*Defense of the Catholic Faith on the Satisfaction of Christ Against Faustus Socinus*	Manifestation not satisfaction of divine justice	Daniel Whitby Samuel Clarke Richard Watson J. McLeod Campbell H. R. Mackintosh
Dramatic	Aulén	*Christus Victor*	Victory of Christ over evil powers	Karl Heim J. S. Whale
Penal substitutionary	Calvin	*Institutes of the Christian Religion*	Penal substitution rendering God propitious toward sinners	Charles Hodge W. G. T. Shedd L. Berkhof A. H. Strong R. W. Dale James Denny P. T. Forsyth K. Barth

of" neither contradict each other nor exclude each other. When we translate both expressions by "for," then this one word signifies a twofold aspect. It is exactly the uniqueness of Christ's act that makes it not an impersonal substitution but one that benefits others.[21]

Two Pauline passages may be especially noted: Galatians 3:13 and Romans 3:21-26. "Christ redeemed us from the curse of the law, having become a curse for us" (Gal. 3:13, ASV). This statement cannot be interpreted to mean anything other than that Christ, the sinless one, took upon Himself the penalty that sinners should have borne, by rights. In the Romans passage (3:21-26) the apostle insists that atonement through the death of Christ shows God to be both just and merciful "God set forth [Christ Jesus] to be a propitiation, . . . for the showing, I say, of his righteousness . . . that he might himself be just, and the justifer of him that hath faith in Jesus" (vv. 25-26, ASV). Leon Morris states, "It is very difficult to see what this means unless it is that Christ has borne our penalty so that God upholds the majesty of the divine law even in the process whereby guilty sinners are forgiven."[22]

Other passages which should be examined include Hebrews 9:26 and 1 Peter 2:24.

Theories of the Atonement

Berkhof, Louis. *The History of Christian Doctrine*. Grand Rapids: Eerdmans, 1937.

Culpepper, Robert H. *Interpreting the Atonement*. Grand Rapids: Eerdmans, 1966.

Mackintosh, Robert. *Historic Theories of Atonement*. London: Hodder and Stoughton, 1920.

ASPECTS OF THE ATONEMENT
A GENERAL ASPECT—OBEDIENCE

The work of Christ is described in Scripture in terms of obedience with sufficient frequency to suggest its appropriateness as a unifying or integrating principle. (Cf. Isa. 52:13-15; John 6:28; 10:17-18; Rom. 5:19; Gal. 4:4; Phil. 2:7-8; Heb. 5:8-9.)

Theologians usually make a distinction between what is termed Christ's *active* obedience and His *passive* obedience.

His *active* obedience means that He obeyed the positive demands of the law. Paul states that He was "made under the law" (Gal. 4:4).

---

21. Berkouwer, 308.
22. Leon Morris, "Penal View of the Atonement," *His,* Dec. 1960, 16.

Christ, being born a Jew, was made under the civil law of the Jews, and to this law He submitted.

He was made under the ceremonial law and became subject to that. He was circumcised when eight days old, according to that law; He was presented in the Temple at the time of His mother's purification, as the law required; at twelve years of age He came with His parents to Jerusalem, to keep the Passover. When He had begun His public ministry, it was His custom constantly to attend synagogue worship. One of the last actions of His life was to keep the Passover with His disciples.

By fulfilling the ceremonial aspect of the law He abolished it; for when it was fulfilled, it was no longer useful.

Christ was also made under the moral law. To fear God and keep His commandments is the whole duty of man, and this was the duty of Christ, as man. But in addition, Christ was made under it, as the surety and substitute of His people.

His *passive* obedience means that He submitted to the penal sanctions of the law. Christ willingly endured all sufferings for the sake of His people; it was the Father's will that He should. He was not rebellious; He neither turned His back away from the smiters nor His face from shame and spitting (Isa. 53:7; 1 Pet. 2:23-24).

SPECIFIC ASPECTS

There are four New Testament words which express distinct facets of salvation in Christ: *sacrifice, propitiation, reconciliation,* and *redemption.* In each of these, man stands in a different relationship before the same God: first as a guilty person, second as an object of God's wrath, third as an enemy, and fourth as a slave.

SACRIFICE

Sacrifice is directed to the need created by our guilt. It is solidly rooted in the Old Testament and is basically (though not exclusively) expiatory in meaning. Sacrifice was a divinely instituted provision whereby sin might be covered and the liability to divine wrath removed. There were certain general characteristics of the Old Testament's sacrifices: (1) the victim was to be without blemish, pointing typically to the sinlessness of Jesus; (2) the offerer was to lay his hands on the victim, looking forward to the acceptance of our guilt by Jesus; (3) the victim was slain, typifying the death of Jesus on the sinner's behalf; and (4) in connection with the peace offering, certain parts were given to the priest and the rest was eaten by the worshipers in a meal of fellowship, prefiguring our fellowship in Christ and with each other.

A FOURFOLD PICTURE OF CHRIST'S SAVING WORK

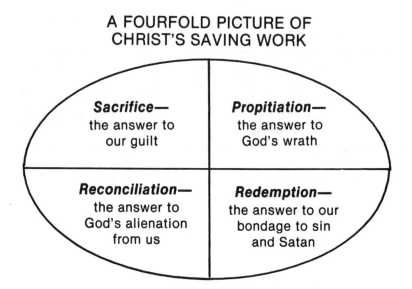

Sacrifice—
the answer to
our guilt

Propitiation—
the answer to
God's wrath

Reconciliation—
the answer to
God's alienation
from us

Redemption—
the answer to our
bondage to sin
and Satan

Biblical Theology of the Atonement

DeVaux, Roland. *Studies in Old Testament Sacrifice.* U. of Wales, 1964. Reprint. Mystic, Conn.: Lawrence Verry, n.d.

Guillebaud, H. E. *Why the Cross?* London: Inter-Varsity, 1946.

McDonald, H. D. *Forgiveness and Atonement.* Grand Rapids: Baker, 1984.

Morris, Leon. *The Cross in the New Testament.* Grand Rapids: Eerdmans, 1965.

Payne, J. Barton. *The Theology of the Older Testament.* Grand Rapids: Zondervan, 1962. Pages 380-94.

The entire New Testament speaks of Christ's death in sacrificial terms, but this is especially emphasized in the epistle to the Hebrews. The writer of this epistle frequently refers to Christ as a high priest, and the primary function of a high priest is to offer sacrifice (Heb. 5:1; 8:3). It is this which distinguishes a priest from other men. The writer further indicates that our great High Priest *must* have something to offer (8:3); and that something was Himself (9:26). He alone could be both priest and victim.

Christ's sacrifice is unique in several respects. It is singular in that it was offered once for all, whereas in the levitical system sacrifices had to be repeatedly offered (9:25). This once-for-all offering has permanent effects (10:12, 14). It is also unique because of it having been offered in heaven, not in an earthly sanctuary (4:14; 9:24). Nothing can be added to such a sacrifice.

Further, Christ's sacrifice is distinctive because it alone has the *inherent* quality to atone for men's sins; animal sacrifices could only do so symbolically as anticipation of Christ's work (10:4). It is also singular because it opened up unlimited access to the very presence of God for all His people (10:19-22). Under the Mosaic economy only the high priest went into the holy place and then only once a year, on the Day of Atonement (9:6-7). It also is unique because it was an active doing of the will of God, not a passive doing of it as in the case of animal sacrifices (10:5-10).

Atonement as Sacrifice

Edersheim, Alfred. *The Temple: Its Ministry and Services as They Were at the Time of Jesus Christ.* London: The Religious Tract Society, n.d.

Gayford, Sydney C. *Sacrifice and Priesthood, Jewish and Christian.* London: Methuen, 1953.

Murray, John. *Redemption: Accomplished and Applied.* Grand Rapids: Eerdmans, 1955. Pages 30-35.

Warfield, Benjamin. *The Person and Work of Christ.* Philadelphia: Presbyterian and Reformed, 1950. Pages 391-426.

PROPITIATION

Propitiation is directed to the need that arises from the wrath of God. The Greek word which is translated as our English word *propitiation* is used only three times in the New Testament (Rom. 3:25; 1 John 2:2; 4:10), though it is common in the Septuagint for our English word *atonement.*

In an effort to ascertain the meaning of propitiation we may note, for one thing, that the concept is expressed in the Hebrew Old Testament by a word which means "cover." This covering takes place in reference to sin; and the effect is cleansing and forgiveness. Both the covering and its effects take place before the Lord (cf. especially Lev. 4:35; 10:17; 16:30).

This latter point stresses the fact that sin creates a situation *in relation to the Lord,* a situation that makes the covering necessary.

The covering is that which provides for the removal of the divine displeasure which the sin evokes.

The concept of God's wrath is written largely in the Old Testament; it is not the exclusive concept of one or two writers but is to be found throughout the entire corpus. This concept stresses the seriousness of sin (Ps. 11:5-7; 97:10; Jer. 44:4). One must be careful here however that he does not conceive of propitiation as that work whereby the Son wins over an incensed Father to clemency and love. Rather, the love of God is the source from which the atonement derives. "God so loved . . . that he gave" (John 3:16).

From a study of the Old Testament data we may state that the divine love and hate are compatible aspects of the divine nature. It should be clear that the divine wrath is not a sudden uncontrolled outburst of passion but rather a fixed, controlled burning anger against sin. It is the righteous revulsion of God's being against that which is a contradiction of His holiness.

We may diagram the doctrine of propitiation as follows:

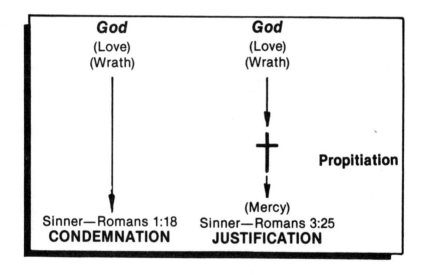

Meaning of Propitiation

Morris, Leon. *The Apostolic Preaching of the Cross.* Grand Rapids: Eerdmans, 1955. Pages 125-85.

Murray, John. *Redemption: Accomplished and Applied.* Grand Rapids: Eerdmans, 1955. Pages 35-39.

Walvoord, John F. *Jesus Christ Our Lord.* Chicago: Moody, 1969. Pages 171-77.

RECONCILIATION

Reconciliation is directed to the need created by God's alienation from us. It presupposes disrupted relations between God and men, an alienation which on our part is caused by sin (Isa. 59:2). Some scholars (T. H. Hughes, Vincent Taylor, Paul Althaus) accept this as the most important way of viewing the atonement, but this would seem difficult to support in light of the infrequency of the term in the New Testament. It is used in only four Pauline passages (Rom. 5:10-11; 2 Cor. 5:18-20; Eph. 2:16; Col. 1:20-21) and is scarcely found outside his writings.

W. H. Griffith Thomas writes on reconciliation:

> This refers to the adjustment of differences by the removal of enmity and separation. There is practical unanimity among scholars that reconciliation in St. Paul means a change of relation on God's part towards man, something done by God for man, which has modified what would otherwise have been His attitude to the sinner. Thus, reconciliation is much more than a change of feeling on man's part towards God, *and must imply first of all a change of relation in God towards man.*[23]

Leon Morris states, "Paul sees the reconciliation as meaning that God does not reckon to men their trespasses."[24]

We briefly examine the two notable Pauline passages on reconciliation: Romans 5:6-11 and 2 Corinthians 5:18-21.

Romans 5:6-11

> While we were still helpless, at the right time Christ died for the ungodly. For one will hardly die for a righteous man; though perhaps for the good man someone would dare even to die. But God demonstrates His own love toward us, in that while we were yet sinners, Christ died for us. Much more then, being justified by His blood, we shall be saved from the wrath of God through the death of His Son, much more, having been reconciled, we shall be saved by His life. And not only this, but we also exult in God through our Lord Jesus Christ, through whom we have now received the reconciliation. (Rom. 5:6-11, NASB)

Paul sets forth Christ's death as a proof of the Father's love—"God demonstrates His own love toward us in that . . . Christ died for us" (v. 8*a*). "This love is at once original and unmerited, for it is extended to those who are completely powerless to help themselves."[25]

Paul indicates that this death reconciled us while we were enemies—

23. W. H. Griffith Thomas, *The Principles of Theology* (London: Church Bk. Rm. Press, 1956), 53.
24. Morris, *The Apostolic Preaching of the Cross* (Grand Rapids: Eerdmans, 1956), 249.
25. Geoffrey B. Wilson, *Romans* (London: Banner of Truth, 1969).

"God demonstrates His own love toward us, in that while we were yet sinners, Christ died for us" (v. 8), "for . . . while were were enemies, we were reconciled to God" (v. 10).

Although the major idea of "enemies" in the context is that men were hostile to God, it also implies a strong reaction on God's part to man's sin. "Seen, then, in the wider context of the New Testament thought, Rom. v. 8-11 may be said to indicate a reconciliation in which there is a Godward as well as a manward aspect."[26]

The meaning of the Greek term would seem to indicate that the work of reconciliation itself has to do with the removal of God's enmity toward fallen man; whereas the change in man's attitude toward God is a result of reconciliation.[27]

Note Godet's comments on this matter:

> Does this word denote man's enmity to God, or that of God to man? Hating God (*dei osores*) or hatred of God (*Deo odiosi*)? The first notion would evidently be insufficient in the context. The enmity must above all belong to Him to whom *wrath* is attributed; and the blood of Christ, through which we have been *justified,* did not flow in the first place to work a change in our disposition Godward, but to bring about a change in God's conduct toward us . . . In our passage the true meaning does not seem to us doubtful. The word *being reconciled* reproducing the *being justified* of ver. 9, it follows from this parallelism that it is God, and not man, who gives up His enmity. In the same way as by justification God effaces all condemnation, so by reconciliation He ceases from His wrath.[28]

2 Corinthians 5:18-21

> Now all these things are from God, who reconciled us to Himself through Christ, and gave us the ministry of reconciliation, namely, that, God was in Christ reconciling the world to Himself, not counting their trespasses against them, and He has committed to us the ministry of reconciliation. Therefore, we are ambassadors for Christ, as though God were entreating through us: We beg you on behalf of Christ, be reconciled to God. He made Him who knew no sin to be sin on our behalf, that we might become the righteousness of God in Him. (2 Cor. 5:18-21, NASB)

Reconciliation is a work of God, not man—"God . . . reconciled us to Himself" (v. 18); "God was in Christ reconciling the world to Himself" (v. 19).

26. Morris, *Cross*, 199.
27. Ibid., 200.
28. F. Godet, *Commentary on the Epistle to the Romans* (Grand Rapids: Zondervan, 1956), 195 ff. For a different view see Gerhard Kittel, ed., *Theological Dictionary of the New Testament,* vol. 1 (Grand Rapids: Eerdmans, 1964), 265 ff.

Reconciliation is a finished work—note the tenses in verses 18, 19, 21. Reconciliation is not something being continuously wrought but rather something decisively accomplished in the past.

Reconciliation has essentially to do with the vicarious sin-bearing of Christ. "He made Him who knew no sin to be sin on our behalf, that we might become the righteousness of God in Him" (v. 21).

Reconciliation is forensic in character. "Not counting their trespasses against them" (v. 19). "Counting" clearly indicates that Paul is thinking legally rather than experientially. Reconciliation is a work of God in Christ whereby He removes the ground of His holy alienation from the sinner and thus does not impute their trespasses against them. The subjective change of the sinner's attitude toward God is a result of the objective work of reconciliation accomplished by Christ.

Christians, as ambassadors of Christ, are to urge sinners to respond in faith to God's work. "Be reconciled to God" (v. 20).

Meaning of Reconciliation

Banks, Robert, ed. *Reconciliation and Hope: New Testament Essays on Atonement and Eschatology.* Grand Rapids: Eerdmans, 1975.

Morris, Leon. *The Apostolic Preaching of the Cross.* Grand Rapids: Eerdmans, 1955. Pages 186-223.

Murray, John. *Redemption: Accomplished and Applied.* Grand Rapids: Eerdmans, 1955. Pages 39-48.

Taylor, Vincent. *The Atonement in New Testament Teaching.* London: Epworth, 1954.

Walwoord, John F. *Jesus Christ Our Lord.* Chicago: Moody, 1969. Pages 177-90.

REDEMPTION

Redemption is directed to the need created by man's bondage to sin. It speaks the language of purchase and ransom. Ransom is the securing of a release by the payment of a price. From what has the sinner been released? From law and from sin.

"Christ redeemed us from the curse of the law, having become a curse for us" (Gal. 3:13, ASV). Without deliverance from this curse we would have no salvation.

Christ delivered us from the relative and provisional bondage of which the Mosaic economy was the instrument. "But now that faith is come, we are no longer under a tutor. For ye are all sons of God, through faith, in Christ Jesus" (Gal. 3:25-26, ASV).

Christ has redeemed us from the necessity of keeping the law as the condition for acceptance by God. "For as through the one man's disobedience the many were made sinners, even so through the obedience of the one shall the many be made righteous" (Rom. 5:19, ASV). *Note:* As Christians we are not released from the obligation to love the Lord our God with all our heart and soul and strength and mind and our neighbor as ourselves—the law is comprehended in these two commandments (Matt. 22:37-40; Rom. 13:10; see also Rom. 8:1-4, and the booklet entitled *The Divine Command,* by Paul Althaus [Philadelphia: Fortress, 1966]).

Redemption from sin embraces the several aspects from which sin may be scripturally viewed. In examining Hebrews 9:11-12 and Revelation 5:9, we note particularly: (1) redemption from guilt—justification and forgiveness of sin (cf. Rom. 3:24; Eph. 1:7; Col. 1:14; Heb. 9:15); (2) redemption from the power of sin—deliverance from its enslaving defilement (cf. Titus 2:14; 1 Pet. 1:18; and (3) redemption from the presence of sin—glorification (Rom. 8:23).

Meaning of Redemption

Guillebaud, H. E. *Why the Cross?* 2d ed. London: Inter-Varsity, 1956.

Morris, Leon. *The Apostolic Preaching of the Cross.* Grand Rapids: Eerdmans, 1955. Pages 186 ff.

Murray, John. *Redemption: Accomplished and Applied.* Grand Rapids: Eerdmans, 1955. Pages 33 ff.

Walvoord, John. F. *Jesus Christ Our Lord.* Chicago: Moody, 1969. Pages 163-71.

EXTENT OF THE ATONEMENT

The extent of the atonement is a matter about which there has been much heated argument and debate; unfortunately, even today segments of the church of Jesus Christ are torn over the issue. From the standpoint of the evangelistic message this unhappy circumstances need not be. Certainly all born-again Christians agree that the Bible teaches that Christ died for sinners, and in the preaching of the gospel this is all that needs to be stated; the question of the designed extent of the atonement need not come into the story at all. We include here a brief discussion of the issue for the sake of completeness.

MAJOR PROTESTANT VIEWS

There are three major views within what may be loosely called Protestantism.

1. *Unrestricted universalism* is the view that God designed to save all

men by the atonement and that in consequence all men will eventually be saved, if not in this life then in the afterlife. This position is largely held by liberals, although there is an evangelical type of universalism.

2. *Qualified universalism* maintains that God planned to save all men by the atonement but that all will not be saved, because of an *ultimate* failure to believe. This view is held largely by Arminians.

3. *Particularism* argues that God purposed by the atonement to save only the elect, and that in consequence only they are saved. This view is held by Calvinists.

THE ISSUE

In respect to the latter two views, the real point of departure arises out of the *nature* of the limitation imposed upon the atonement. John Murray rightly states, "Whether the expression 'limited atonement' is good or not we must reckon with the fact that unless we believe in the final restoration of all men we cannot have an unlimited atonement. If we universalize the extent we limit the efficacy."[29]

William G. T. Shedd has given an excellent analysis of this problem. He correctly differentiates between a passive and an active signification of the term *extent*. The word *extent* in a passive sense is equivalent to *value*. Shedd states, "In this use of the term, all parties who hold the atonement in any evangelical meaning would concede that the extent of the atonement is unlimited. Christ's death is sufficient in value to satisfy eternal justice for the sins of all mankind."[30]

In an active sense, however, "extent" denotes the act of extending. "The 'extent' of the atonement, in this sense, means its personal application to individuals by the Holy Spirit. The extent is now intent."[31] Hence the question really is, To whom is the atonement effectually extended? The scriptural answer to this question is, The elect. In this specific sense therefore the atonement is limited. "Writers upon the 'extent' of the atonement have sometimes neglected to consider the history of the word, and misunderstanding has arisen between disputants who were really in agreement with each other."[32]

Summarizing the discussion thus far, we state that in the passive

---

29. John Murray, *Redemption: Accomplished and Applied* (Grand Rapids: Eerdmans, 1955), 64.
30. Ibid.
31. Ibid.
32. Ibid.

sense of the term *extent*, we refer to the intrinsic value of the atonement, which must be viewed as *unlimited;* in the active sense we refer to its intended application, which must be viewed as *limited* to the elect.

An additional significant distinction to be made in this discussion relates to the difference of meaning between atonement and redemption. The latter includes the *application* of the atonement. "It is the term 'redemption' not 'atonement' which is found in those statements that speak of the work of Christ as limited by the decree of election." (See Heb. 2:17; Eph. 1:14; 2:8-9; etc.) For this reason in the *Westminster Confession* it is properly said that "to all those for whom Christ hath purchased *redemption*, he doth certainly and effectually apply and communicate the same."

In *The Canons of the Synod of Dort* we read with respect to value: "The death of the Son of God is the only and most perfect sacrifice and satisfaction for sin; is of infinite worth and value, abundantly sufficient to expiate the sins of the whole world." With respect to intent: "For this was the sovereign counsel and most gracious will and purpose of God the Father, that the quickening and saving efficacy of the most precious death of his Son should extend to all the elect."[33]

J. Oliver Buswell correctly states,

> There is no question among those who adhere to the Calvinistic system of doctrine as to the fact that the atonement of Christ is universal in three respects: (1) It is *sufficient* for all. It is absolutely infinite in its value and thus in its potentiality . . . (2) The atonement is *applicable* to all. There is nothing lacking in the mode of Christ's incarnation or in His death and resurrection which would make it inapplicable to any member of the human race in any earthly circumstances. (3) The atonement is *offered* to all.[34]

The specific issue revolves around the question of design, or intent, of the atoning work of Christ. From Scripture it would appear that it is the specific intention of the Father to purchase through the death of His Son the salvation of the elect: "He will save *his people* from their sins" (Matt. 1:21, KJV; cf. Isa. 53:8; Luke 1:68); "I lay down my life for *the sheep*" (John 10:15; KJV; cf. v. 29); "He prophesied that Jesus should die . . . [to] gather into one *the children of God* that are scattered abroad" (John 11:51-52, ASV); "Greater love has no one than this, that one lay down his life for his *friends*" (John 15:13, NASB);

33. Philip Schaff, *The Creeds of Christendom* (New York: Harper, 1877), 586-87.
34. J. Oliver Buswell, *A Systematic Theology of the Christian Religion* (Grand Rapid Zondervan, 1962), 141 ff.

"Christ . . . loved *the church,* and gave himself for it" (Eph. 5:25, ASV); "The Son of man came . . . to give his life a ransom *for many*" (Matt. 20:28, ASV; cf. Matt. 26:28; Mark 10:45); "Jesus Christ . . . gave himself *for us*" (Titus 2:14, ASV).

Now, it must be admitted that these references do not in themselves exclude others, of the nonelect, from the saving benefit of Christ's atoning death; but all of the passages certainly indicate that the relationship of His redeeming work to those who are saved is different from that which it bears to those who are lost.

Consistency demands that the twofold aspect of Christ's priestly work be viewed as harmonious; that the sacrifice and intercession be coextensive. From John 17:9, the intercession of Christ appears to be explicitly restricted to the saved. He says, "I am not praying for the world now, but only for those whom you have given me, because they are yours" (*Williams*). It would seem incredible that Christ does not pray for some for whom He died. (Cf. Isa. 53:12; Rom. 8:34; 1 John 2:1-2).

The objects of election and redemption are the same. Paul states, "Who will bring a charge against God's elect? . . . Christ Jesus is He who died" (Rom. 8:33-34, NASB). Christ died for the elect. Election and redemption are of equal extent; no more are redeemed by Christ than are chosen in Him.

Certain passages (e.g., Ezek. 33:11; John 3:16; 1 Tim. 2:4; 2 Pet. 3:9) are set forth as teaching a universal saving will of God. However, these passages do not necessarily mean that God's *decretive* will is for the salvation of all men without exception. They indicate the general benevolence of God toward fallen man, revealing that He takes special delight in the salvation of the sinner. They cannot be said to fairly prove more.

By the expression "all men" in 1 Timothy 2:4 (KJV), we would understand "some of all sorts throughout the world." Context argues for the correctness of this view. After stating in verse 1 that supplications and prayers are to be made for all men, Paul immediately proceeds, in verse 2, to explain what he means by "all men"—all classes of men, even those in high places of authority.

Again, in 2 Peter 3:9 we find expressed God's patience toward all of fallen mankind. In the gospel God makes His loving-kindness known to all alike, but He only grasps those (effectually calls those) whom He chose before the foundation of the world. We must remember that a sovereign God desires, or has pleasure in the accomplishment of, what He does not necessarily decretively will.

Other passages are pointed to as teaching that some for whom Christ died may perish. These verses include Romans 14:15; 1 Corinthians 8:10-11; Hebrews 10:29; and 2 Peter 2:1.

Romans 14:15 does not teach that the "weaker brethren" will ultimately perish. The apostle instructs the "stronger brethren" to exercise their Christian freedom responsibly toward those of weaker faith, lest they cause the later to sin. Compare 1 Corinthians 8:10-11; this would seem to refer to the destruction of the weaker brother's peace and comfort for a time.

Hebrews 10:29 and 2 Peter 2:1 both refer to what the apostates *professed* to have, rather than to what they had in fact. By their lives they denied the very Lord whom they professed had bought them.

Finally, some passages are presented as implying that the work of Christ was designed for all men. Verses cited include John 12:32; Romans 5:18; 2 Corinthians 5:14-15; 1 Timothy 2:6; and 1 Timothy 4:10. Actually, John 12:32 teaches, in the light of the context (vv. 20 ff.), that Christ will draw peoples from among all nations to Himself—Gentiles as well as Jews. This text speaks of men collectively rather than distributively.

Romans 5:8 teaches, in the light of the context of the entire epistle, that one man's act of righteousness leads to acquittal and life for all men; that is, for all who are of the elect (8:33), and who therefore believe (5:17). The free gift of Christ's righteousness comes on all to justification, that is, on all who are the spiritual seed of Christ, and on no one else. Likewise, the "us all" of Romans 8:32 must be understood, on the basis of the context, as those who have been elected (cf. 8:28-29).

When viewing its immediate context, we seek that 2 Corinthians 5:14-15 teaches that Christ died for those who are viewed as in Christ, for those who are a new creation (v. 17), for those who are reconciled (v. 18).

First Timothy 2:6 cannot be understood as meaning each and every individual man, for then either all would be ransomed (universalism) or else the ransom price would be paid in vain, at least for some. This passage should be understood in respect to the "many" as spoken of by Christ in Matthew 20:28, "to give his life a ransom for many." The apostle's "all" is best understood as indicating that the Gentiles, as well as the Jews, were included in the benefits of Christ's death.

There are various interpretations of 1 Timothy 4:10. The *universalistic* view maintains that all men will eventually be saved; none will finally be lost. The special sense in which God is Savior of believers is found in the fact of their enjoying earlier the blessings of salvation. The biblical doctrine of eternal punishment refutes this view.

In the *providential* view the term *Savior* is taken to mean preserver. God saves all men by giving them life, by sending them sunshine and rain and fruitful seasons. The special sense in which God is Savior of believers is found in the fact that they enjoy in the highest degree what all men enjoy to a limited degree. The problem with this view is that it overlooks the spiritual aspects of salvation which are clearly expressed in the context.

The *potential-actual* view argues that God is the Savior of all men in that He desires and therefore provides in Christ salvation for all. This potential universal salvation becomes actual only to those who believe. The problem with this view is that the adverb *specially* would ordinarily mean that all men must enjoy to some degree what believers are said to enjoy in the highest degree. Obviously such a requirement is not met in this interpretation.

The *temporal-eternal* view maintains that God's savlation is one. As applied to non-Christians, it includes their preservation in this life and the enjoyment of certain blessings which come to man by common grace. As applied to believers, however, this salvation extends into eternity. This view would seem to be the best one, because it gives the proper force to the word *specially*. Further, it is in agreement with the temporal-eternal elements of the context (e.g., 4:8), and it employs the word *Savior* in an adequate way.

Extent of the Atonement

Berkhof, Louis. *Vicarious Atonement Through Christ.* Grand Rapids: Eerdmans, 1936.

Boettner, Loraine. *The Atonement.* Grand Rapids: Eerdmans, 1941.

Douty, Norman F. *The Death of Christ.* Irving, Tex.: Williams and Watrous, 1978.

Long, Gary D. *Definite Atonement.* Philadelphia: Presbyterian and Reformed, 1976.

"The Nature and Extent of the Atonement." *Bulletin of the Evangelical Theological Society 10,* no. 4 (Fall 1967). This subject is dealt with from the Lutheran, Wesleyan, and Reformed perspectives.

4

The Application of Salvation

WE NOW TURN OUR ATTENTION to what theologians term the *ordo salutis,* the order of the application of Christ's redeeming work, the way of salvation (see Appendix A). It should be understood at the outset that this order is logical rather than temporal. From a temporal perspective these individual acts occur simultaneously.

CALLING

We do not refer to vocational calling in this area of our study. Every legitimate occupation of life is in a significant sense a calling of God (1 Cor. 7:20, 24), but the calling under consideration is of a soteriological kind. As we are presently using it, calling is the *initial* saving act of God. This would seem to be clearly implied from Paul's order in Romans 8:30. The scriptural doctrine of redemptive calling is twofold in aspect.

THE GENERAL CALL

The general call is a call which comes through the proclamation of the gospel: it is a call which urges sinners to accept salvation. "On the last day, the great day, of the feast, Jesus stood and cried aloud, 'If anyone is thirsty, let him come to me and drink' " (John 7:37, Williams; cf. Matt. 11:28; Isa. 45:22; etc.).

This message (kerygma), which is to be authoritatively pro-claimed—not optionally debated—contains three essential elements: (1) It is a story of historical occurrences—an historical proclamation: Christ died, was buried, and rose (1 Cor. 15:3-4). (2) It is an authorita-tive interpretation of these events—a theological evaluation. Christ died for our sins. (3) It is an offer of salvation to whosoever will—an ethical summons. Repent! Believe!

The general call is to be freely and universally offered. "Jesus came up [to the disciples] and said, 'Full authority in heaven and on earth has been given to me. Go then and make disciples of all the nations' " (Matt. 28:18-19, *Williams*).

THE EFFECTUAL CALL

The effectual call is efficacious; that is, it always results in salvation. This is a *creative* calling which accompanies the external proclamation of the gospel; it is invested with the power to deliver one to the divinely intended destination. "It is very striking that in the New Testament the terms for calling, when used specifically with reference to salvation, are almost uniformly applied, not to the universal call of the gospel, but to the call that ushers men into a state of salvation and is therefore effec-tual."[1]

Perhaps the classic passage on the effectual call is found in Romans 8:30: "Whom he did predestinate, them he also called" (KJV). Other pertinent references include: Romans 1:6-7; 1 Corinthians 1:9, 26; 2 Peter 1:10.

The efficacious call is immutable, thereby insuring our perseverance. "For the gifts and the calling of God are irrevocable" (Rom. 11:29, NASB).

This is a call which is a high, holy, and heavenly calling. God "saved us and called us with an holy calling" (2 Tim. 1:9, KJV; cf. Heb. 3:1).

The *efficient* cause of the effectual call is God the Father. "God is faithful, by whom ye were called unto the fellowship of his Son Jesus Christ our Lord" (1 Cor. 1:9, KJV; cf. Rom. 8:30; Gal. 1:15; Eph. 1:17-18; 2 Tim. 1:9, etc.).

The *moving* cause, as we have seen, is the sovereign will and pleasure of God. He called us "in accordance with his own purpose" (2 Tim. 1:9, *Williams*). It is His determinate purpose which moves Him to call by His grace.

---

1. John Murray, *Redemption: Accomplished and Applied* (Grand Rapids: Eerdmans, 1955), 88.

The *instrumental* cause is the ministry of the word. "Sometimes, indeed, it is brought about by some remarkable providence, and without the word; but generally it is by it: Faith comes by hearing, and hearing by the word of God."[2] Paul said of the Thessalonians, "He called you through our preaching of the good news, so that you may obtain the glory of our Lord Jesus Christ" (2 Thess. 2:14, *Williams*).

As the gospel is proclaimed, the general call goes forth and God in accordance with His sovereign elective purpose causes it to become effectual in the lives of some. Charles H. Spurgeon relates in his autobiography his own conversion and speaks forcefully of the difference between the general and the efficacious call.

> The general call of the gospel is like the sheet lightning we sometimes see on a summer's evening—beautiful, grand—but who ever heard of anything struck by it? But the special call is the forked flash from heaven; it strikes somewhere. It is the arrow shot in between the joints of the harness.[3]

Those who receive the effectual call are brought out of gross darkness into marvelous light. "You are the chosen race, the royal priesthood, the consecrated nation, the people called to be His very own, to proclaim the perfections of Him who called you out of darkness into his wonderful light" (1 Pet. 2:9, *Williams*). "Darkness" here means ignorance—about God's perfections, purposes, counsels, and methods of grace, and about one's own fallen state and condition. Through the illumination of the Spirit one is brought into a life-transforming knowledge of God's grace.

These individuals are called out of bondage into liberty. "You, brothers, were called to freedom; only you must not let your freedom be an excuse for the gratification of your lower nature, but in love be slaves to one another" (Gal. 5:13, *Williams*). While in a state of nature, one is enslaved to sin and Satan; but in the effectual call one is set free from these dreadful shackles and bidden to stand fast in the liberty with which Christ has set him free, serving others in love.

They are also called into fellowship with Christ. "God is faithful, by whom ye were called unto the fellowship of his Son Jesus Christ our Lord" (1 Cor. 1:9, KJV). The Christian is one who has been effectually called to fellowship *in* and/or *with* Christ—the genitive may be either objective or subjective. Certainly both ideas are true.

---

2. John Gill, *A Body of Doctrinal Divinity* (Atlanta: Turner Lassetter, 1957), 543.
3. Charles Haddon Spurgeon, *The Early Years: 1834-1859* (London: Banner of Truth, 1962), 72.

They are called to peace. "God hath called us to peace" (1 Cor. 7:15, KJV). This is a call to peace of mind and conscience; to a flourishing state of soul. This peace involves our relationship with God, ourself, and our fellow man.

They are called out of a state of unholiness into holiness. "For God called us not for uncleanness, but in sanctification" (1 Thess. 4:7, ASV; cf. 1 Pet. 1:15). Contextually the unholiness referred to is in the realm of sexual matters, but this statement would be equally true in all areas of life.

They are called into the grace of Christ. Paul writes to the Galatians, "I am amazed that you are so quickly deserting Him who called you by the grace of Christ" (Gal. 1:6, NASB).

They are called into a state of happiness and bliss in another world. God calls believers into His own kingdom and glory (1 Thess. 2:12; cf. John 17:22; Col. 3:4; 1 Tim. 6:12; 1 Pet. 5:10).

The distinction between these two aspects of God's calling may be pictorially represented.

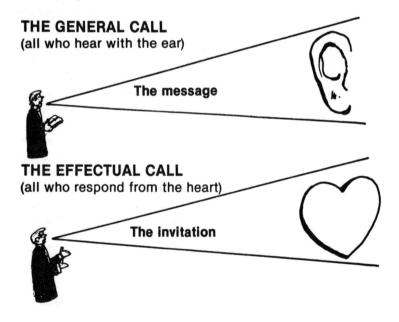

THE GENERAL CALL
(all who hear with the ear)

The message

THE EFFECTUAL CALL
(all who respond from the heart)

The invitation

REGENERATION

It is God the Father who, as we observed, calls His own out of the kingdom of darkness into the kingdom of light; but the sinner must do the coming. And yet, if one is *dead* in trespasses and sin, how may he answer this divine call? This spiritual dilemma is movingly described by Octavius Winslow. He writes of the awful picture of the unrenewed state of man represented under the biblical image of *death.* This spiritual dilemma is analogous to the utter futility of a doctor's efforts to revive the corpse of one of his patients. We may preach the terrors of hell or the blessings of heaven with great eloquence but a spiritually dead man cannot respond.

The believing response which the call of the gospel requires is a moral and spiritual impossibility. "They that are in the flesh cannot please God" (Rom. 8:8, KJV). Christ Himself clearly stated, "No one can come unto me, except it were given unto him of my Father" (John 6:65, KJV; cf. v. 44). How then, we ask, may this inability to respond be overcome? Only one answer may be given. It is the glory of the gospel of God's sovereign grace that it overcomes this dilemma. God's call, when it is effectual, carries with it the operative grace necessary to enable the person called to respond in faith to the Savior. This grace is the grace of regeneration.

MEANING OF REGENERATION

The noun *regeneration* occurs in Scripture only twice. In Matthew 19:28 it is used eschatologically to denote the renewal of the world prior to the coming of the kingdom; and in Titus 3:5, it is used soteriologically, perhaps denoting baptism as the sign and seal of regeneration.

The reality of regeneration is often referred to in different words and images. It is expressed by the phrase *born again.* Jesus said to Nicodemus, "Truly, truly, I say to you, unless one is born again, he cannot see the kingdom of God" (John 3:3, NASB; cf. v. 7; 1 Pet. 1:3, 23). This language presupposes a first birth to which regeneration is the second. Note the following contrasts between the two:

The First Birth	*The Second Birth*
a. Of sinful parents	a. Of God
b. Of corruptible seed	b. Of incorruptible seed
c. Of the flesh—carnal	c. Of the Spirit—spiritual
d. Satan's slave	d. Christ's free man
e. An object of divine wrath	e. An object of divine love

In John 3, we read of the meeting of Nicodemus with Jesus. Nicodemus was a leader in the orthodox religious party of his day, but he was unregenerate. On this occasion he desired to see Jesus in order to discover the secret of entry into the kingdom of God (the redemptive rule of God). But even before he had opportunity to express what was in his mind, Jesus provided the answer to his question: A man may not so much as see the kingdom unless he is born again. It is divinely necessary that he be sovereignly regenerated by the Spirit of God.

Verse 5 presents the problem of the meaning of "water." Jesus said, "Truly, truly, I say to you, unless one is born of water and the Spirit, he cannot enter into the kingdom of God" (NASB). Four views may be briefly mentioned. (1) The water is that of John's baptism and is symbolic of repentance. From the standpoint of historical context this view would seem to commend itself. (2) The water reflects a Jewish usage which sees it as denoting the male semen. If this is accepted, then we have two alternative ways of interpreting the passage. The expression *born of water* may be taken as either *born of natural birth* or *born of spiritual seed*. (3) The water is that of Christian baptism. The meaning then would be that a man must be baptized and also born of the Spirit if he is to enter the kingdom. Respecting this view the Catholic scholar Raymond E. Brown correctly states, "If the phrase 'of water,' were part of the original form of the discourse, then it would have been understood by Nicodemus against the O.T. background rather than in terms of Christian Baptism."[4] (4) The water is a symbol for the Word of God. J. C. Macaulay writes, "The explanation most satisfying to my own mind is that which, linking Scripture with Scripture, sees the water as a figure of the Word."[5] The weakness in this view is that it involves an interpolation of Paul's usage of this figure into Christ's conversation with one who is indoctrinated with Old Testament concepts, not Pauline. It would seem therefore that either of the first two views would fit most adequately into the context. In connection with this problem one should also examine Ezekiel 36:25-26. The prophet states,

> I will sprinkle clean water upon you, and ye shall be clean: from all your filthiness, and from all your idols, will I cleanse you. A new heart also will I give you, and a new spirit will I put within you; and I will take away the stony heart out of your flesh, and I will give you a heart of flesh. (ASV)

4. Raymond E. Brown, *The Gospel According to John (i-xii),* The Anchor Bible, vol. 29 (New York: Doubleday, 1966), 1428.
5. J. C. Macaulay, *Devotional Studies in St. John's Gospel* (Grand Rapids: Eerdmans, 1954, 46.

This passage would suggest that *water* is purificatory and *spirit* renovatory.

Regeneration may possible be called being *born from above*. Jesus' words to Nicodemus may be translated "born from above" (John 3:3, 7, *Williams*; cf. James 1:17-18). The author of this birth is from above; those who are born again are born of their Father who is in heaven.

Regeneration is called "renewal of the Holy Spirit" (Titus 3:5, *Williams*); it results in "a new creation" (2 Cor. 5:17, *Williams*), in "the new self" (Eph. 4:24, *Williams*). The people who are regenerated are referred to as "newborn babes" (1 Pet. 2:2, NASB).

It is regeneration that is meant by the phrase *being quickened*. "And you hath he quickened, who were dead in trespasses and sins" (Eph. 2:1, KJV; cf. v. 5; cf. also John 6:63; Rom. 8:1-10). As there is a quickening time in natural generation, so there is in regeneration. In the most definitive scriptural sense *regeneration* denotes that act of God whereby spiritually dead men are quickened (made alive) through the Spirit. By this act God plants the principle of a new spiritual life in the soul; one is born again. Regeneration in this limited sense is solely a work of God. Hence the words of Christ to Nicodemus, "You must be born again" (John 3:7, NASB), point not to a moral obligation but to a divine necessity.

PROPERTIES OF REGENERATION

Regeneration is a passive work—men can no more contribute to their spiritual birth than infants can to their natural birth. John Owen correctly states, "The natural and carnal means of blood, flesh, and the will of man, are wholly rejected in this matter; and the whole efficiency of the new birth is ascribed to God alone."[6] Regeneration is always ascribed to the Holy Spirit as the efficient cause (John 3:3-6).

It is an irresistible work—one could no more resist this work than he could his own resurrection or an infant could its own generation. The work of the Spirit is like the wind which blows where it wills and none can hinder it (John 3:8). An unwilling people are made willing in the day of His power.

Regeneration is an instantaneous work—it is not like progressive sanctification, which is carried on gradually. As an infant is generated

---

6. John Owen, *A Discourse Concerning the Holy Spirit* (Philadelphia: Presb. Bd. Pub., n.d.), 121.

at once and not by degrees, so it is in spiritual generation. No man can be said to be more regenerated than another, though he may be more sanctified.

It is a mysterious work—no man can really understand this wondrous work of God's grace. The work of the Spirit is like the wind; "You do not know where it comes from or where it goes" (John 3:8, *Williams*).

A FURTHER OBSERVATION

The term *regeneration* is often used more broadly to denote "the *entire* change by grace effected in our persons, ending in our dying to sin in death and our being born for heaven."[7]

Calvin identified repentance with regeneration, thus taking regeneration to be a *conscious response* to God's grace whereby one is being restored to God's image. He wrote, "In a word, I interpret repentance as regeneration, whose sole end is to restore in us the image of God that had been disfigured and all but obliterated through Adam's transgression."[8] He cites such passages as 2 Corinthians 3:18; Ephesians 4:23; and Colossians 3:10, continuing, "Accordingly, we are restored by this regeneration through the benefit of Christ into the righteousness of God; from which we had fallen through Adam. In this way it pleases the Lord fully to restore whomsoever he adopts into the inheritance of life."[9]

Perhaps it would be best to employ the term *quickening* for what has been generally understood to be regeneration in a *limited* sense and thereby preserve the term *regeneration* for something of what Kuyper, Calvin, and most present-day evangelicals suggest.

Regeneration

Buchanan, James. *The Office and Work of the Holy Spirit.* London: Banner of Truth, 1966.

Burkhardt, Helmut. *The Biblical Doctrine of Regeneration.* Translated by O. R. Johnston. Downers Grove, Ill.: Inter-Varsity, 1978.

Kuyper, Abraham. *The Work of the Holy Spirit.* Grand Rapids: Eerdmans, 1946.

---

7. Abraham Kuyper, *The Work of the Holy Spirit* (Grand Rapids: Eerdmans, 1946), 193.
8. John Calvin, *Institutes of the Christian Religion,* Library of Christian Classics, vol. 20, ed. John Baillie, John T. McNeill, Henry P. Van Deusen (Philadelphia: Westminster, 1960), 601.
9. Ibid.

Owen, John. *The Holy Spirit, His Gifts and Power.* Grand Rapids: Kregel, 1954.
Ryrie, Charles Caldwell. *The Holy Spirit.* Chicago: Moody, 1965.

CONVERSION

The Hebrew and Greek terms for conversion mean basically "to turn" and in the world of religious thought denote a change of outlook and a new direction in life and action.

Conversion involves a turn both toward and away from something or someone.

MEANING OF CONVERSION

Positively, faith is turning toward something or someone. In the soteriological dimension it is a turn *toward* God. Paul "kept declaring both to those of Damascus first, and also at Jerusalem and then throughout all the region of Judea, and even to the Gentiles, that they should repent and turn to God" (Acts 26:20; NASB; cf. 9:35; 11:21; 15:19; 1 Pet. 2:25).

This turn, or act of faith, may be defined as an understanding of and mental assent to certain basic facts concerning the person and work of Christ culminating in a committal of one's entire being to the person of whom those facts testify. Three important elements are to be noted in this definition.

1. *Knowledge.* We must know who Christ is, what He has done, and what He is able to do (1 Cor. 15:3-4). Apart from such knowledge, faith would be blind conjecture at the best and foolish mockery at the worst. We are not called to put faith in someone of whom we have no knowledge. Saving faith is not a blind leap in the dark.

2. *Assent.* We must not only know the truth respecting Christ; we must also believe it to be true. It is possible, of course, to understand the import of certain propositions of truth and yet not believe these propositions. In saving faith, truths know are also accepted as true.

3. *Trust.* Knowledge of and assent ot the truth of the gospel is not saving faith. They must be accompanied by trust in the person of Jesus Christ. Christian faith is not merely intellectual assent to the divinely revealed propositions of Scripture; it must include commitment to Christ. Strictly speaking it is not even faith in Christ that saves, but Christ who saves through faith.

Genuine faith must grasp special revelation in its twofold aspect: (1) the written word and (2) the personal word. The former has to do with the knowledge content of faith, the latter with the communion content; the former with doctrine, the latter with experience. The former is objective, the latter is subjective. The former without the latter leads to a cold, empty intellectualism; the latter without the former leads to a confused and meaningless mysticism. Both together lead to a normal Christian experience.

We may diagram the dynamic elements of faith as follows:

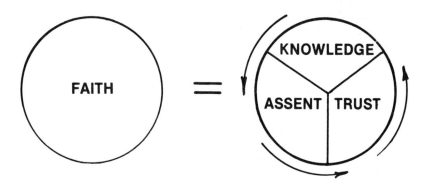

Negatively, repentance is turning away from something or someone. The biblical terms for repentance suggest a change of mind, of judgment, purpose, and conduct. Repentance denotes properly a change for the better, a change of mind that is durable and productive of good conduct.

Repentance is the gift of God, the purchase of Christ, and the work of the Holy Spirit. "God has granted . . . the repentance that leads to life" (Acts 11:18, NASB). It is implanted by the Spirit at regeneration, or quickening.

It is also an abiding principle. "The man who does not see his need of exercising repentance daily may have a counterfeit, but cannot have a true repentance."[10] The Bible teaches not only the necessity of an initial conversion of the sinner but also subsequent conversion of erring saints.

Repentance includes a godly sorrow for sin. The remorse of the truly penitent involves a deep contrition of heart, not so much for the punishment to which he is exposed as for the indignity he has done to a holy and gracious God. Paul styles this "Sorrow in accordance with the will of God," as in contrast to worldly sorrow (2 Cor. 7:10, *Williams;* see also Ps. 51:4).

10. John Colquhoun, *Repentance* (London: Banner of Truth, 1965), 28.

Repentance is a turning from idols (1 Thess. 1:9). Historically, Paul literally meant graven images; by application to us, we should understand that an idol is anything which comes between man and his creator, whether a person, place, thing, or idea. Repentance is also a turning from vain things (Acts 14:15), from darkness (26:28*a*), and from the power of Satan (26:18*b*).

One of the most helpful passages on conversion is Psalm 119:59-60: "I thought on my ways, and I turned my feet unto thy testimonies. I made haste, and delayed not to keep thy commandments" (KJV; cf. Luke 15:17, 20; 1 Thess. 1:9). From this passage we learn several important ideas.

First, as a *preparation for conversion,* there must be *careful introspective reflection either on one's ways or on God's;* the psalmist wrote, "I thought on my ways" (KJV), or "thy ways" (RSV). Sometimes God works in providentially drastic ways to bring man to seriously contemplate his course of life. Recall the prodigal son (Luke 15:17); it was only after he found himself in a pigsty that he began to think on his course of behavior. In application of this passage John Colquhoun writes,

> Survey minutely your inclinations and thoughts, your words and actions, even from your earliest years. Put to yourself seriously such questions as these: What have I been intending and pursuing all these days? What has been the rule of my conduct? the maxims of men, or the Word of God? the customs of the world, or the example of Christ? What has the supreme love of my heart been fixed on? Have I given to Christ, or to the world, my strongest desires and warmest attachments? Has it been my habitual intention to please God, or to please myself? Has it been His glory that I have aimed at in every pursuit, or my own gratification, wealth or honour?[11]

If men are to be converted, they must be brought to think carefully about their ways and about God's ways toward them.

Second, as *an act of converting* there must be *a decisive turning toward the one of whom the Word testifies.* Again, the psalmist wrote, "I turned my feet unto thy testimonies." The emphasis in the biblical doctrine of conversion is upon the positive response of faith—a turning *to* God in Christ.

> Though the graces of faith and repentance are, in respect of time, implanted together and at once; yet in order of nature, the acting of faith goes before the exercise of true repentance. The sinner then must cordially

---

11. Ibid., 23.

believe or trust in Christ for pardon, in order to exercise evangelical mourning for sin, and turning from it unto God. True repentance is very pleasing to God, "but without faith, it is impossible to please him" (Heb. 11:6).[12]

Here again the prodigal furnishes us with an illustration of the meaning of true conversion; he not only thought on his ways but he also rose and returned to his father's house (Luke 15:20).

Third, as an *evidence of conversion* there must be obedience. Finally, the psalmist wrote, "I made haste . . . to keep thy commandments." True conversion means a changed life. "Hereby we do know that we know him, if we keep his commandments" (1 John 2:3, KJV). The cost of discipleship is obedience to our Master. "True penitents turn . . . to their duty to God as their Lord and Master. When Saul of Tarsus became a penitent, he said, 'Lord what wilt Thou have me to do?' All who return to God come home as servants to do His work. All who become His friends do whatsoever He commands them (John 15:14). They 'delight in the law of God after the inward man,' and have respect to all His commandments."[13]

Dietrich Bonhoeffer wrote forcefully of the necessity for obedience to Christ as an evidence of true conversion. He stated,

> Cheap grace is the deadly enemy of our Church. We are fighting today for costly grace . . . Cheap grace is the preaching of forgiveness without requiring repentance, baptism without church discipline, Communion without confession, absolution without personal confession. Cheap grace is grace without discipleship, grace without the cross, grace without Jesus Christ, living and incarnate.
>
> Costly grace is the gospel which must be *sought* again and again, the gift which must be *asked* for, the door at which a man must *knock*.
>
> Such grace is *costly* because it calls us to follow, and it is *grace* because it calls us to follow *Jesus Christ*.[14]

G. I. Williamson summarizes and illustrates the doctrine of conversion:

> Repentance and faith are two aspects of this full-orbed transformation of the soul. Repentance denotes that aspect of change whereby the soul turns from sin and experiences true abhorrence of it. Faith denotes that aspect of change whereby the soul turns to Christ and experiences supreme attachment to him. Both phases of this complete turning involve the total personality—reason, affections, and will. We may diagram this as follows:

12. Ibid.
13. Ibid.
14. Dietrich Bonhoeffer, *The Cost of Discipleship* (New York: Macmillan, 1949), 35 ff.

CONVERSION

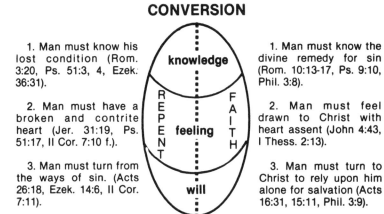

1. Man must know his lost condition (Rom. 3:20, Ps. 51:3, 4, Ezek. 36:31).

2. Man must have a broken and contrite heart (Jer. 31:19, Ps. 51:17, II Cor. 7:10 f.).

3. Man must turn from the ways of sin. (Acts 26:18, Ezek. 14:6, II Cor. 7:11).

1. Man must know the divine remedy for sin (Rom. 10:13-17, Ps. 9:10, Phil. 3:8).

2. Man must feel drawn to Christ with heart assent (John 4:43, I Thess. 2:13).

3. Man must turn to Christ to rely upon him alone for salvation (Acts 16:31, 15:11, Phil. 3:9).

(The dotted line indicates that there is no hard and fast break between repentance and faith.)[15]

MEANS OF CONVERSION

The means of conversion are efficient, moving, and instrumental. The *efficient* cause is *God,* not man. The drastic alteration brought by conversion is not in man's power to effect—an Ethiopian might just as well try to change his skin or a leopard his spots; such things are impossible (Jer. 13:23; see also Rom. 9:16; John 1:13). John Gill rightly states,

> Conversion is the motion of the soul towards God; but as this cannot be in a dead man, and unless he is quickened, so not unless he is drawn by efficacious grace; wherefore God in conversion draws men with loving kindness to himself; and, with the cords of love, to his Son; for no man, says Christ, can come unto me, except the Father, which hath sent me, draw him. (John 6:44).[16]

The *moving* cause is the good will of God. This is the same as is the moving cause of regeneration and effectual calling; it is not the merits of men—we obviously have none (1 Cor. 6:9-11; Eph. 2:3-4).

The *instrumental* cause is the ministry of the Word. Though in the most unusual circumstances conversion may be wrought without the Word by some remarkable act of providence, generally it is brought

15. G. I. Williamson, *The Westminster Confession of Faith for Study Classes* (Philadelphia: Presb. & Ref., 1964), 97 ff.
16. Gill, 549.

about through the preaching and teaching of the Word. "Faith cometh by hearing, and hearing by the word of God" (Rom. 10:17, KJV; cf. Gal. 3:2; see also 1 Cor. 3:5).

It should be carefully noted that the preaching of the Word is not sufficient of itself to produce the work of conversion in the heart. Men may hear it and yet not be converted by it. Its proclamation must be accompanied by the power and demonstration of the Spirit.

This is made clear in Paul's statements in 1 Corinthians 2:1-5.

> And I, brethren, when I came to you, came not with excellency of speech or of wisdom, declaring unto you the testimony of God. For I determined not to know any thing among you, save Jesus Christ, and him crucified. And I was with you in weakness, and in fear, and in much trembling. And my speech and my preaching was not with enticing words of men's wisdom, but in demonstration of the Spirit and of power: that your faith should not stand in the wisdom of men, but in the power of God. (KJV)

The power of Paul's preaching is seen by a careful consideration of both his *message* and his *method*. The words *of God* (v. 1) may be taken either as a subjective or an objective genitive. If the former, Paul would simply mean the testimony which goes forth from God; if the latter, the testimony which has God as its object. Although we cannot be sure which nuance was intended in this statement, we may assert that both ideas are biblically true. The apostle held a mandate from God and he spoke of no one else but God. (A textual note: In the place of "testimony" some other ancient authorities read "mystery"—the Greek words are somewhat similar in spelling.)

"Jesus Christ and him crucified" (v. 2). Paul deliberately determined that among the Corinthians he would know only the one great central truth of the person and work of Jesus Christ, with special focus on the event of the crucifixion. The crucifixion is the heart of the gospel; it is by His death on the cross that sinners are redeemed.

Thus, Paul's message was the testimony from God and/or to God concerning the person and work of His Son, Jesus Christ.

"I came not with excellency of speech or of wisdom" (v. 1). Paul did not come to the Corinthians with oratorical flurry or philosophical subtlety, though he would have been amply capable of both.

"And my speech and my preaching was not with enticing words of man's wisdom" (v. 4). Paul probably did not intend to differentiate between "speech" and "reaching" with any exactness. Rather, he likely employed both terms to indicate both the message he preached and the way he preached it. One thing seems clear, regardless of how we interpret the meaning of these two words: the main thrust of Paul's statement is to disclaim any confidence in rhetorical phrases and rational demonstrations. This he had also done earlier in 1:17, "For Christ sent me . . . to preach the gospel: not with wisdom of words, lest the cross of Christ should be made of none effect" (KJV).

An important word of caution needs to be sounded here lest there be an unfortunate misinterpretation of Paul. The apostle certainly had no objection to persuasive words or logical thought per se; he was a master of both—for the former, note 1 Corinthians 13 and for the latter, the epistle to the Romans. The point is, however, that he would not allow either to operate as an end in itself but only as an instrument to be employed under the guidance of the Spirit for the interpretation and communication of divine revelation.

"And I was with you in weakness and in fear, and in much trembling" (v. 3). The expression *in weakness* is probably best understood to refer to the apostle's physical condition. "Possibly the malady which had led to his first preaching in Galatia (Gal. iv. 13) was upon him once more. If this was epilepsy, or malarial fever (Ramsay), it might well be the recurrent trouble which he calls a 'thorn for the flesh' (II Cor. xii. 7)."[17]

The words "in fear, and in much trembling" probably speak of his psychological frame of mind. He was properly fearful for the success of the ministry of the Word among the Corinthians. In his heart attitude the apostle was not carnally confident but spiritually dependent.

"Declaring" (v. 1). The word *kataggellein* means "to announce" or "to proclaim," but the chief emphasis in the word is on the *authoritative* nature of the proclamation. This is one of the great New Testament words for preaching. From its usage therein, we learn that preaching is not the proclamation of a preacher's private opinions, nor the public airing of his doubts, but rather the full authoritative proclamation of the Word of God.

"And my speech and my preaching was in demonstration of the Spirit and of power" (v. 4). Verse 4 presents a sharp contrast. The apostle would seem to be saying, "I did not make it my work to demonstrate gospel propositions to you through neat words and phrases, nor from principles of natural reason *but* in demonstration of the Spirit and of power." The words "in demonstration of the Spirit and of power" could be either an objective or a subjective genitive. If objective, then Paul means a demonstration which has for its object the

17. Archibald Robertson and Alfred Plummer, *A Critical and Exegetical Commentary on the First Epistle of St. Paul to the Corinthians,* International Critical Commentary (Edinburgh: T & T Clark, 1914), 31.

presence or working of the Spirit and power. If subjective, he means the demonstration (of the truth) which springs from the Spirit and power of God. It would seem that the subjective use is preferable. It may be noted that F. F. Bruce has taken it as a subjective gentitive in his paraphase of Paul's epistles. He renders it, "None the less, it was attended by the powerful conviction produced by the Spirit."[18]

The term *demonstration* speaks of the most rigorous form of proof. In the papyri it is used of official evidence or proof.

> In [*demonstration*] the premises are known to be true, and therefore the conclusion is not only logical, but certainly true . . . St. Paul is not dealing with scientific certainty: but he claims that the certitude of religious truth to the believer in the Gospel is as complete and as "objective"—equal in degree, though different in kind—as the certitudes of scientific truth to the scientific mind. Mere human [wisdom] may dazzle and overwhelm and seem to be unanswerable . . . ; it does not penetrate to these depths of the soul which are at the seat of the decisions of a lifetime.[19]

Godet writes,

> The word [*demonstration*] indicates a clearness which is produced in the hearer's mind, as by the sudden lifting of a veil; a conviction mastering him with the sovereign force of moral evidence; comp. xiv. 24, 25.—The gen . . . "of Spirit," is the complement of cause; it is the Divine Spirit alone who thus reveals the truth of salvation; comp. Eph. 1:17, 18 . . . [Paul] was not ignorant that a faith, founded on logical arguments, could be shaken by other arguments of the same nature. To be solid, it must be the work of the power of God, and in order to be that, proceed from a conviction of sin and a personal appropriation of salvation, which the Spirit of God alone can produce in the human soul. The preacher's task in this work lies, not in wishing to act in the place and stead of the Spirit with the resources of his own eloquence and genuis, but in opening up the way for Him by simple testimony rendered to Christ.[20]

Paul's preaching was a clear authoritative proclamation of the simple gospel. But precisely because it was so simple and unpretentious, its results demonstrated the power of God. Sinners were converted to Christ. Thus our preaching, teaching, and witnessing will be effective to the degree to which they center in the gospel of Jesus Christ and rely

18. F. F. Bruce, *The Letters of Paul, An Expanded Paraphrase* (Grand Rapids: Eerdmans, 1965), 71.
19. Robertson and Plummer, 33.
20. F. Godet, *Commentary on the First Epistle of St. Paul to the Corinthians* (Grand Rapids: Zondervan, 1957), 129-30.

upon the powerful demonstration of the Spirit of God (see 1 Thess. 1:5; 2:13).

This communication of the message may be by monologue (Acts 15:7) or dialogue (6:9-14; 9:22, 29; 17:2-3; 18:4; 19; 19:8-9; 24:25; 28:23; note esp. 18:27-28). Much of the ministry of the early preachers was done in discussion and debate.

Conversion

Alleine, Joseph. *The Alarm to the Unconverted.* London: Banner of Truth, 1959.

Barclay, William. *Turning to God: A Study of Conversion in the Book of Acts and Today.* London: Epworth, 1963. Reprint. Philadelphia: Westminster, 1964.

Brandon, Owen. *Christianity from Within.* London: Hodder and Stoughton, 1965.

Howe, Reuel L. *Partners in Preaching.* New York: Seabury, 1967.

Johnson, Cedric B. *Christian Conversion: Biblical and Psychological Perspectives.* Grand Rapids: Zondervan, 1982.

Stott, John R. W. *Our Guilty Silence.* Grand Rapids: Eerdmans, 1969.

THREE BIBLICAL CASES OF CONVERSION
LYDIA (ACTS 16:13-15)

> On the Sabbath day we [Paul and Barnabas] went outside the gate of the city by the riverside, where we supposed that there was a place of worship and, when we sat down, we talked to the women who gathered. One woman, named Lydia, a purple-seller from the city of Thyatira, a worshiper of God, listened, and the Lord opened her heart to give attention to the things that Paul spoke. (Acts 16:13-14, *New Berkeley*)

It is true that, unlike a pagan Gentile, Lydia was a proselyte to the Jewish faith, a believer in the one true God. But despite her genuine piety she needed to be converted, and that is the fact which should be clearly understood from this passage.

The narrative implies that although Lydia was a devout proselyte to the Jewish faith, her heart was still shut against the reception of the truth as it is in Jesus. When the text states that "the Lord opened her heart," the implication is that her heart was in such a state that, apart from the gracious operation of the Holy Spirit, it would have remained closed to the gospel message.

The term *heart* means the whole moral nature of man, including the understanding, conscience, will, and affections. In this comprehensive sense her heart was closed against the reception of the truth as it is in Christ. Only God's sovereign grace could remove this obstacle.

Today many resemble Lydia, being ever so conscientious and devout according to their light, but still ignorant and unbelieving with respect to the gospel.

Although the text does not explicitly state so, from our understanding of New Testament truth we may understand that there was a direct personal operation of the Spirit on the heart of Lydia. He moved those obstacles which otherwise obstructed the admission of the truth. Paul could not effect this change in Lydia's heart. It was while the apostle was preaching (that is, as the general call of the gospel was going forth) that the Spirit worked decisively in Lydia's heart—"The Lord opened her heart." Only God can open the heart of the sinner to the reception of Christ as Savior and Lord.

While only the Lord can open the heart—through the Holy Spirit—He employs the truth as conveyed through words as the instrument of conversion. "The Spirit's agency does not supersede the use of the Word: on the contrary, the truth read or heard is still the wisdom of God, and the power of God, unto salvation."[21] Luke states, "The Lord opened her heart to give attention to the things that Paul spoke."

As the Spirit of the Lord worked mightily in her heart she responded in faith, was baptized, and extended Christian hospitality to her missionary friends. Lydia's faith is seen by love to Christ and deeds of kindness to His servants.

Practical lessons form this case

1. It shows the care with which God provided for the saving instruction of earnest seekers in the Jewish community.

2. It shows the importance of prayer as a divinely ordained means of spiritual advancement.

3. It shows the necessity of a decisive spiritual change in the lives of those who are religious but not Christian.

4. It provides a clear indication of the interrelated functions of the Word and the Spirit in the work of conversion.

5. It reinforces the duty of combining diligence in the use of means with depending upon the Spirit for divine blessing.

THE PHILIPPIAN JAILER (ACTS 16:19-34)

> "Sirs, what must I do to be saved?" They said, "Believe on the Lord Jesus and you will be saved, and your family also." Then they told him, together with his whole family, the word of the Lord.

21. James Buchanan, *The Office and Work of the Holy Spirit* (London: Banner of Truth, 1966), 190.

At that very hour of the night the jailer took them and washed their wounds; and he was baptized then and there, he and all that were his. Then, taking them up to his house, he set food before them and was extremely happy with all his loved ones because they had believed in God. (Acts 16:30-34, *New Berkeley*)

The Philippian jailer despaired of his life when he saw the situation which had been brought about through the earthquake. "For a man brought up to a Roman soldier's ideas of duty and discipline there was only one course open—suicide."[22]

He became a concerned sinner (v. 29). Here we see a change of attitude from initial total despair to an anxious inquiry. By God's grace the jailer was brought under deep concern for his soul. He was convicted by the Spirit of his danger and the need of salvation. (It should be noted that his question was interpreted by the apostles as having reference to his spiritual condition. From the human perspective this conviction of need is likely accounted for by what he had heard and seen since the apostles had come to Philippi.)

At this point, however, although the jailer had moved from desperation to conviction he was not yet converted. "He was only at the stage of conviction which precedes conversion, but which is not always followed by it."[23] Although he had deep fear he did not yet have faith. "He had an awful apprehension of danger; but danger may be apprehended while the method of deliverance is unknown."[24]

That he was not yet converted at that point is evident from his question "Sirs, what must I do to be saved?" This question indeed implies that he was now convinced of his danger, concerned for his soul, and impressed with the necessity of salvation; but it also indicates that as yet he was ignorant of the method of deliverance. The wording of the question might suggest that he had a legalistic answer in mind. He asked, What must I *do?* not, How may I obtain? "The first impulse of every convinced sinner, before he is savingly converted, is to look to some efforts or doings of his own as the means of his deliverance"[25]—reformation of life, deeds of charity, or some other outward observance.

While the outward circumstances surrounding conversion vary with each individual, the *means* is always one and the same; it is nothing other than the truth as it is in Jesus, the full and free offer of the gospel.

22. F. F. Bruce. *Commentary on the Book of Acts,* New International Commentary on the New Testament (Grand Rapids, Eerdmans, 1954), 337.
23. Buchanan, 135.
24. Ibid.
25. Ibid.

When this man came to the apostles saying, "Sirs, what must I do to be saved?" they immediately replied, "Believe in the Lord Jesus." And this word accompanied by the power of the Spirit was the means whereby this convicted sinner became a converted man.

Note the nature of the message. It centered in Christ—"Believe in the Lord Jesus." The name "Lord" speaks of Christ as the highly exalted one, the sovereign; the name "Jesus," of Christ as the Savior of His people. Also, the message encompassed an appeal to his whole house—"and your family."

It is clear that the jailer's conversion consisted in his responding to the apostles' exhortation (vv. 32-34). Luke states, "He . . . was extremely happy with all his loved ones because they had believed in God" (v. 34).

The jailer extended hospitality to these missionaries by washing their wounds and preparing food for them; thus, his works served as evidence of his conversion. His fears had been removed and now he could really enjoy life. Finally, by being baptized, he made an open profession of his faith.

Practical lessons form this case.

1. God can shake the sinner out of his spiritual apathy by some awakening stroke of providence. It may not be by an earthquake, but it may be by calamity of some other sort. "Many a Christian may trace his first serious impressions to a season of personal or domestic trial."[26]

2. This awakening will result in conviction of spiritual need and a quest for the answer, as the Spirit works in the heart.

3. The gospel, which is divinely designed to provide the answer to the sinner's sense of need is the only effectual instrument of conversion.

4. *Conviction* ends in *conversion* only when a true sense of sin is combined with a belief in the Lord Jesus Christ.

5. Conversion by the Word through the Spirit produces good works.

PAUL (ACTS 9:1-28)

On [Pauls'] journey, as he neared Damascus, a light from Heaven suddenly blazed around him, and he fell to the ground. Then he heard a voice speaking to him,

"Saul, Saul, why are you persecuting me?"

"Who are you, Lord?" he asked.

"I am Jesus whom you are persecuting," was the reply. "But now stand up

---

26. Ibid.

and go into the city and there you will be told what you must do." (Acts 9:3-6, Phillips; cf. 22:1-21; 26:4-18; see also Gal. 1:13; 1 Cor. 15:9)

Before his conversion, Paul was a man of great intellectual attainment. He was a staunch Jew in both his religious opinions and his moral habits (Acts 26:4-5; Gal. 1:14; Phil. 3:4-6). He was a violent, sincere persecutor of the Christian church. Paul had "a zeal for God, but not according to knowledge" (Rom. 10:2, ASV; cf. Acts 26:9; Phil. 3:6; 1 Tim. 1:13).

There were several preternatural accompaniments to Paul's regeneration. These were: the light from heaven, "far brighter than the sun" (Acts 26:13, Phillips); the voice from heaven; and Paul's blindness, which was miraculously cured (9:17-18). It should be clearly understood that these striking circumstances were useful in arresting Paul's attention and in impressing on his conscience his spiritual need—but it was the truth itself, the simple truth as it is in Jesus, which effected Paul's conversion.

His conversion was brought about by the communication of the truth through the *vision* and *voice* of the Savior and the ministry of Ananias, made effective in the heart by the demonstration of the Spirit.

Paul's vision of Christ proved as well as exhibited the truth of the gospel. This vision showed that Christ had indeed risen from the dead and ascended to the right hand of the Father. It demonstrated that His work had been accepted and that He was truly the anointed of the Father; that He was therefore to be worshiped and served.

While the truth was personally embodied in the vision of Christ, it was further explained by His *voice*. The words of the triumphant Jesus brought forcefully to Paul's heart the fact that in fighting the gospel he had been fighting against God. It is therefore no wonder that Paul lay on the earth trembling and astonished! The question which Jesus asked was calculated to awaken Paul's conscience, to reprove him of sin.

But fear is not faith; remorse is not repentance; nor is there sufficient power in mere terror to effect the conversion of the heart. The heart is turned by the attraction of the Saviour's love; and if, on the one hand, the words of Christ served to impress his mind with a very awful sense of his guilt, seeing that they represented his persecution of the Church as equivalent to the persecution of Christ himself, they were also fitted, on the other hand, to convey to his mind a very vivid idea of the tenderness of his compassion and the riches of his grace.[27]

27. Ibid.

God employed the ministry of Ananias to further instruct and confirm Paul in the faith (vv. 6-19).

Practical lessons from this case

1. A man may be learned and outwardly exemplary in life and yet be utterly destitute of spiritual life, needing to be renewed and converted.

2. A man may have a zeal for God which is not according to knowledge; sincere but wrong.

3. Ignorance of the gospel, combined with adherence to some religion and a decent moral life, often issues in an inveterate opposition to Christ.

4. When believed, the truth that Jesus is the Christ lays a solid ground for the sinner's hope.

5. A persecutor may become a preacher.

5

The Results of Salvation

JUSTIFICATION

MEANING OF JUSTIFICATION

IN THE PRIMARY SENSE, justification is concerned not with our spiritual *condition* but with our spiritual *relation;* it is not a matter of our actual *state* but of our judicial *position.*

This true relation was lost by sin. In respect to our relation to God, there are three results of this sin: guilt, condemnation, and separation (note Gen. 3).

Justification is the restoration of this true relation to God, and it includes: removal of guilt by the imputation of Christ's righteousness (Rom. 8:33, KJV: "Who shall lay anything to the charge of God's elect?"); removal of condemnation by the gift of forgiveness (v. 34, KJV: "Who is he that condemneth?"); and removal of separation by the restoration to fellowship (v. 35, KJV: "Who shall separate us?").

Justification is more than pardon. The change effected in man's relation to God may be considered in two distinct aspects: actual justification and a declarative justification. "Actual justification" means that a sinner is *constituted* righteous by having Christ's righteousness imputed to him. Only in this way may a just God justify the ungodly. "Declarative justification" means that a sinner is *declared* righteous before God.

Certain proofs for the forensic, or judicial, sense of the term

63

justification may be noted. First antithetic expressions: In Scripture *justification* is invariably set over against *condemnation*. See, in respect to judgments of men, Deuteronomy 25:1; Proverbs 17:15; and Isaiah 5:23. In these passages, and many others, two judicial sentences are mentioned which are directly the reverse of each other. See, in respect to judgments of God, Matthew 12:37; Romans 5:16; and Romans 8:33-34. Second, correlative terms: These designate one or the other of the various circumstances which are implied in a process of judgment. (See Gen. 18:25; Ps. 32:1; Rom. 2:2, 15; 8:33; 14:10; Col. 2:14; 1 John 2:1.) And third, equivalent expressions: See Romans 4:3, 6-8; 2 Corinthians 5:19, 21.

James Buchanan aptly states, respecting the two aspects of justification (actual and declarative),

> While there is a real analogy, there is also an important difference, between the divine act of justification, and the judicial procedure of human courts. The sentence of a human judge is merely *declarative;* it does not constitute a man either innocent or guilty, it only pronounces him to be so in the eye of the law: it may even be erroneous, and may pronounce one to be innocent who is really guilty, and another to be guilty who is really innocent; whereas in justifying a sinner, God does what no human judge can do,—He first constitutes him righteous, who was not righteous before, and then declares him to be righteous in His infallible judgment, which is ever according to truth. It is chiefly in its *declarative* aspect that the divine act of justification is analogous to the sentence of a human judge; and the difference between the two cases consists in the one having respect to a vicarious, the other to a personal, righteousness; while both are forensic or judicial, as being pronounced with reference to a law or rule of righteousness, which is applicable to each of them respectively.[1]

Justification is to be distinguished from sanctification.

Note: Roman Catholic theology has historically confused justification with sanctification.

FOUNDATION OF JUSTIFICATION

From the positive viewpoint, the basis of our justification is God's grace as manifested in our Lord's perfect life of obedience and His sacrificial death. His spotless righteousness and the whole merit of His divine person and atoning work form the ground of our justification. We are justified by His blood (Rom. 5:9). His righteousness is imputed to us (Rom. 4:6; 1 Cor. 1:30; 2 Cor. 5:21).

---

1. James Buchanan, *The Doctrine of Justification* (London: Banner of Truth, 1961), 248.

JUSTIFICATION "Christ *for* us"	SANCTIFICATION "Christ *in* us"
a. Our standing	a. Our state
b. Our position	b. Our condition
c. Relationship	c. Fellowship
d. Our peace—Christ for us	d. Our purity—Christ in us
e. Acceptance	e. Attainment
f. No degree— instantaneous	f. Subject to degrees— progressive

What Paul is concerned to make clear is that God has accomplished in Christ what man is unable to do for himself and that what He had done is quite unmerited, unprompted, and unsought. This is the essence of grace (Rom. 3:24). The point is that our justification depends wholly on God and not on anything in ourselves.

From the negative viewpoint, it is absolutely impossible for human works to form the basis of justification, for our obedience to the law is impossible (Rom. 3:28; Gal. 2:16). God requires perfect obedience (Gal. 3:10) and this, man cannot render.

Two reasons for justification without the works of the law may be specifically noted: (1) assurance of the forgiveness of sins (Rom. 4:16); and (2) glorification of God rather than self (Eph. 2:8-9; 1:6-7).

Scripture not only teaches that justification is without works; it also denounces those who would teach or believe contrary to this. Study carefully the following references from Paul's epistle to the Galatians: 1:8-9; 2:21—3:3, 10; 5:4.

METHOD OF JUSTIFICATION

"How can man be just with God?" (Job 9:2, ASV). Many hundreds of years ago Job asked this fundamental question; only God can answer it.

The word of the gospel is the medium of justification; justification of the sinner is pronounced in the word of the gospel. In other words, as near as the word of faith is to us, so near to us is God's acquittal.

The merit of our Lord becomes ours "through faith" (Eph. 2:18, KJV; cf. Acts 13:39). Paul states, "But now apart from Law the righteousness of God has been manifested being witnessed by the Law and the Prophets; even the righteousness of God through faith in Jesus Christ for all who believe" (Rom. 3:21-22, NASB).

It is important to understand that faith is never the ground of justification, but only its means or channel; it is the hand which simply reaches out to accept the gift.

G. C. Berkouwer writes.

> Nowhere does faith take on the guise of a work, of human achievement which in one way or another effectualizes justification. The prepositions *through (dia)* and *of* or *by (ek)* point us to the way in which man is granted salvation in Christ. In Gal. 2:16, *through faith* and *of faith* are parallel. The shading in terminology offers no real difficulty, since no preposition is ever used with such a grammatical case of the noun *faith* as to render necessary a translation like *because of* or *by reason of* faith. Faith is never put forward as a work of creativity, of mediacy, or merit. It is never given as a ground of justification.[2]

J. Gresham Machen writes,

> The faith of man, rightly conceived, can never stand in opposition to the completeness with which salvation depends upon God; it can never mean that man does part, while God merely does the rest; for the simple reason that faith consists not in doing something but in receiving something. To say that we are justified by faith is just another way of saying that we are justified not in slightest measure by ourselves, but simply and solely by the One in whom our faith is reposed.[3]

Faith is man's positive answer to God's justifying grace. Faith is the correlative of promise. Trust answers to truth. As Hooker has said, "God doth justify the believing man, yet not for the worthiness of his belief, but for His worthiness Who is believed."[4]

VALUE OF JUSTIFICATION

Justification is necessary for spiritual health. It is the foundation of *peace* with God (Rom. 5:1). It is also the foundation of *freedom* in Christ. This means freedom from enslavement to sin and freedom to be concerned for others. When one is released from anxiety about himself, he is able to use his life for others.

It also means freedom to enjoy all the good things of life within the content of the principle of love for others (Rom. 14).

2. G. C. Berkouwer, *Faith and Justification, Studies in Dogmatics,* vol. 3 (Grand Rapids: Eerdmans, 1962), 80.
3. J. Gresham Machen, *What Is Faith?* (Grand Rapids: Eerdmans, 1962), 172.
4. W. H. Griffith Thomas, *The Principles of Theology* (London: Church Bk. Rm. Press, 1956), 192.

Justification

Berkouwer, G. C. *Faith and Justification.* Grand Rapids: Eerdmans, 1954.

Boehl, Edward. *The Reformed Doctrine of Justification.* Grand Rapids: Eerdmans, 1946.

Buchanan, James. *The Doctrine of Justification.* London: Banner of Truth, 1961.

Colquhoun, Frank. *The Meaning of Justification.* London: Tyndale, 1962.

Kung, Hans. *Justification.* New York: Nelson, 1964.

McDonald, H. D. *Forgiveness and Atonement.* Grand Rapids: Baker, 1984.

Owen, John. *Justification By Faith.* Evansville, Ind.: Sovereign Grace, 1959.

ADOPTION

A subject may be acquitted by his sovereign from charges laid against him; yet such actions do not make him the sovereign's son. If he is adopted it must be by a distinct act of favor. Thus we now turn our attention to this aspect of Christ's redeeming work.

MEANING OF ADOPTION

This sonship is not to be equated with the relationship that Christ sustains to the Father as the only begotten Son.

Nor is it to be equated with the relationship that all men sustain to God as His sons by creation. This relationship is referred to in Acts 17:25-29; Hebrews 12:9; and James 1:18. See also Malachi 2:10—although this statement may only indicate God's fatherhood over His ancient people.

The doctrine of adoption is exclusively Pauline. The Greek word rendered "adoption" in our English versions (*huiothesia*) occurs only five times in Scripture and then only in Paul's writings. Once it is applied to Israel as a nation (Rom. 9:4); once to its full realization at the future coming of Christ (Rom. 8:23); and three times as a present reality in the life of the Christian (Rom. 8:15-16; Gal. 4:5; Eph. 1:5).

In Romans 8:15 it is probably best to understand the Spirit of adoption as the Holy Spirit. (Note the parallelism with Gal. 4:6 as an argument for this view.) The Holy Spirit is not the one who adopts—this is more eminently the work of the Father—but He, the Spirit, is the one through whom the child of God is able to cry, "Abba Father," and exercise the rights and privileges of God's child. The repetition "Abba

Father" suggests the confident intimacy which the Holy Spirit produces in the child of God. In Galatians 4:5 Paul indicates that God's purpose is twofold: redemption and adoption. It was God's aim not simply to release slaves but to make sons. In Ephesians 1:5 (ASV) Paul states that God "foreordained" (marked us out in advance) as those who were to receive the honored status of sons.

There has been much discussion as to whether the root of Paul's use of the term *adoption* is Jewish, Greek, Roman, or some other tradition. To this author it would seem to have been more likely Roman. Francis Lyall argues that although a common legal link of Jewish law may be attributed to these three epistles, it appears that Jewish law did not contain a concept of adoption to which the apostle might significantly refer.

> On the other hand Roman law does, and Roman law is a common factor. The churches of Ephesians and Galatians were situated in centers of population, each with Roman authority present, and the church in Rome would certainly know its local law. Taken with Paul's other uses of concepts known to Roman law, a pattern begins to emerge. Paul was a Roman citizen, and also a lawyer trained in Jewish law. It is well-known today that traveling lawyers tend to pick up knowledge of systems other than that of their training, and I find it hard, for this reason alone, to hold that Paul did not know the Roman law. Add to that the fact that Roman law was the system having paramount jurisdiction over him as a citizen, and the case is very strong indeed.
>
> Lastly, . . . the appropriateness of the metaphor must be taken into account. It is unnecessary to speculate which form of adoption, *adoptio* or *adrogatio,* may have been intended. While it is true that *adrogatio* in Paul's time could take place only at Rome, nevertheless both forms have the same fundamental effect. The adoptee is taken out of his previous state and is placed in a new relationship with his new *paterfamilias.* All his old debts are canceled, and in effect he starts a new life. From that time the *paterfamilias* owns all the property and acquisitions of the adoptee, controls his personal relationships, and has rights of discipline. On the other hand he is involved in liability by the actions of the adoptee and owes reciprocal duties of suport and maintenance.
>
> The Christian doctrines of election, justification, and sanctification imply that the believer is taken out of his former state, and is placed in a new relationship with God. He is made part of God's family forever, with reciprocal duties and rights. All his time, property, and energy should from that time forth be brought under God's control. The Roman law of adoption, with its concept of *patria potestas* inherent in it, is a peculiarly useful illustration of these doctrines in action. I conclude that Paul's use of the term "adoption" in Romans, Ephesians, and Galatians was a deliberate, considered, and appropriate reference to Roman law.[5]

5. Francis Lyall, "Roman Law in the Writings of Paul—Adoption," *Journal of Biblical Literature,* 88, 4 (Dec. 1969), 465 f. For a presentation of the Jewish view, seek D. J. Theron, *The Evangelical Quarterly,* 28 (1965): 6 ff.

In the act of adoption a child is taken by a man from a family not his own, introduced into a new family, and regarded as a true son, entitled to all the privileges and responsibilities belonging to this relation.

The reality of this adoption in the spiritual sense may be described as follows: (1) Fallen mankind are strangers to the family of God; enemies to Him, to His law and to all His interests. They are of their father the devil. (2) From this situation they are invited to come and enter His family; to take His name upon them; to share in His parental care and discipline. (3) Such as accept this invitation are received into His family and become entitled to His parental love. From this point they are called the children of God. From this period, they are permitted, and required, to address Him as their Father.

DISTINCTIVENESS OF ADOPTION

It is helpful to compare adoption to other acts of grace already studied.

Adoption may not be separated from regeneration and justification. Those given the right to become sons of God are those born of God (John 1:13). Those who are the recipients of sonship are always those who have been justified.

Adoption, like justification, is a judicial act. It is the bestowal of a status, not the implanting of something within us. It has to do with a relationship, not a disposition.

Adoption is made recognizable and practical by the ministry of the Spirit (Rom. 8:15-16; Gal. 4:6).

Regeneration is the prerequisite of adoption. As Murray states, "When God adopts men and women into his family, he insures that not only may they have the rights and privileges of his sons and daughters but also the nature or dispositions consonant with such a status. This he does by regeneration."[6]

EFFECTS OF ADOPTION

One becomes the recipient of the compassion and care of his heavenly Father (Luke 11:11-13). "The redeemed are brought into a near relation to God; nearer than that of mere intelligent creatures, in proportion to the greatness of the things which have been done and suffered to bring it into being."[7]

---

6. John Murray, *Redemption: Accomplished and Applied* (Grand Rapids: Eerdmans, 1955), 166.
7. Timothy Dwight, *Theology Explained and Defended in a Series of Sermons* (London: Baynes & Son, 1822), 2:181.

God provides sustenance for His children. "The Lord is my shepherd; I shall not want" (Ps. 23:1, KJV).

He also protects them. "Blessed be the Lord, my Rock, . . . my Fortress, my lofty Stronghold, my Deliverer, my Shield in whom I have taken refuge" (Ps. 144:1-2, *New Berkeley*).

He instructs them. "This work he accomplishes by his providence, by his word, by his ordinances, by his ministers, by the life and conversation of Christians, by the divine example of his Son and by the peculiar communications of his Spirit."[8]

He corrects them. "It is for discipline that you endure; God deals with you as with sons; for what son is there whom his father does not discipline?" (Heb. 12:7, NASB; cf. vv. 5-11).

One has access to God with boldness. He may come to Him as a child to a father (Heb. 4:14-16).

One becomes increasingly conformed to the image of Christ, looking forward to that day when the sons of God shall be like Him and see Him as He is (1 John 3:1-2).

One becomes an heir of God and a joint-heir with Christ (Rom. 8:17).

Adoption

McDonald, H. D. *Salvation*. Westchester, Ill.: Crossway, 1982.

Theron, Daniel J. " 'Adoption' in the Pauline Corpus." *Evangelical Quarterly* 28 (1956): 6-14.

Webb, Robert Alexander. *The Reformed Doctrine of Adoption*. Grand Rapids: Eerdmans, 1947.

SANCTIFICATION

This area of our study centers on what is probably the most directly and immediately relevant aspect of the *Ordo Salutis*. "Holiness . . . is a practical concept, and has to do with our present earthly life, rather than with some future heavenly existence."[9] When a man has been converted from the realm of spiritual death to spiritual life he naturally asks how he may best live out that new life. In asking such a question, the subject of biblical ethics emerges as an important aspect of the doctrine of sanctification; this is, therefore, included in the discussion which ensues.

---

8. Ibid., 185.
9. K. F. W. Prior, *The Way of Holiness* (Chicago: Inter-Varsity, 1967), 8.

FOUNDATION OF SANCTIFICATION

Sanctification has to do with the progressive outworking of the new life implanted by the Holy Spirit in *regeneration*.

The indicative of justification leads to the imperative of sanctification; justification is the theological base of evangelical ethics. It may be diagrammed as follows:

JUSTIFICATION	SANCTIFICATION
"Gift" (Indicative) "Good fruits" Declaration (Gal. 5:19-24)	"Task" (Imperative) "Good works" Duty (Gal. 5:25)

It should be noted that in the Pauline writings, expositions of the doctrine of justification are generally followed by exhortations to action. Christians are to live out in fact what has been given them by grace. It is not good works which make a good man, but a good man who does good works.

MEANING OF SANCTIFICATION

The basic meaning of *holy* is "separated," or "set apart." As referring to God we may distinguish between majestic holiness and ethical holiness.

Majestic holiness means God as separate from His creatures. He is infinitely exalted above His creation; He is the transcendent one, wholly-other (Ex. 15:11; Isa. 40:26; 57:15).

Ethical holiness means God as separate from sin. "God cannot compromise with sin in any form. He must demand conformity with His moral laws, and anyone who would have dealings with Him must be pure in thought, word and deed."[10] (See Ps. 24:3-4; Isa. 6:1-5; Heb. 1:12.) Both aspects of God's holiness are reflected in Isaiah 6. If man reacts to God's majestic holiness with a feeling of his creatureliness, then his reaction to God's ethical holiness must bring a consciousness of sin. That which made the prophet tremble before the Lord was not only the consciousness of his finiteness in the presence of the Infinite, but also—and perhaps even more especially—the consciousness of his sin in the presence of moral purity (v. 5).

---

10. Ibid.

It is this ethical aspect of God's holiness that provides the basis for our understanding of the doctrine of sanctification. Sanctification may be defined as "the work of God's free grace, whereby we are renewed in the whole man after the image of God, and are enabled more and more to die unto sin, and live unto righteousness."[11]

"Sanctification is the claiming of all human life and being and activity by the will of God for the active fulfillment of that will."[12] Sanctification "is the universal renovation of our natures by the Holy Spirit, into the image of God, through Jesus Christ."[13] (See 2 Cor. 5:17.)

In 1 Thessalonians 5:23, Paul prays that God would sanctify the Thessalonians throughout. The reason for this prayer is evident from the context. He had enjoined them to the cultivation of certain graces and the exercise of certain duties, and these could only be realized through the work of God upon them. Thus he writes, "May the God of peace Himself make you holy through and through. May your whole being—spirit, soul, and body—be kept blameleess at the coming of our Lord Jesus Christ" (*New Berkeley*).

This text shows that the author of this sanctification is God. This is emphatically expressed—"the God of peace Himself." If God does not do it, no other can. He does it out of His grace, by His own power, and for His own glory.

The Father is here described as "the God of peace" because sanctification is an effect of that peace with Himself which He has made for us by Jesus Christ. John Owen has well stated, "It is holiness that keeps up a sense of peace with God, and prevents those spiritual breaches which the remainders of our enmity would occasion."[14]

The verse also demonstrates that in scope this sanctification includes our whole nature—spirit, soul, and body.

In surety sanctification involves our preservation in the day of judgment. Paul's thought here (1 Thess. 5:23) seems to concern preservation in (*en*) that day itself, not unto (*eis*) that day. At that time we shall be guarded by God Himself. "Be kept" (KJV, "be preserved") is a passive voice; thus the emphasis is on the fact that *He* is the one who shall do the keeping. God not only preserves us blameless *to* the Parousia but He shall also do such *in* that day.

---

11. Ibid.
12. Karl Barth, *Church Dogmatics* (New York: Scribner, 1956), 4:101.
13. John Owen, *The Holy Spirit, His Gifts and Power* (Grand Rapids: Kregel, 1954), 230.
14. Ibid., 220-21.

NATURE OF SANCTIFICATION

The sanctification of the Spirit must not be confused with other important ideas. It does not consist in a conformity to the light of nature, nor in mere external conformity to the law of God, nor in mere outward reformation of life (e.g., the Pharisee).

It does not reside in restraining grace, either. One may be restrained from the grosser sins by the regulations of parents, the laws of magistrates, and the ministry of the Word; he may be providentially preserved from the pollutions of the world, and yet not be sanctified.

It does not lie in gifts, ordinary or extraordinary. Judas Iscariot may well have had both the ordinary gifts of a preacher and the extraordinary gifts of an apostle, and yet he was clearly not a holy man. John Gill writes, "Gifts are not grace; a man may have all gifts, and all knowledge, and speak with the tongue of men and angels, and not have grace; there may be a silver tongue, where there is an unsanctified heart."[15]

Sanctification may be viewed as consisting in putting off the old man and putting on the new (Eph. 4:22, 24). The old man is the corrupt nature with which all men enter this world. By "putting off," the apostle does not mean its destruction but its displacement from the center of control. The new man is the holy nature, wrought in the soul in regeneration. By "putting on," the apostle means the exercise of the graces of which this new nature consists (see Col. 3:12-13).

It is probably best to understand the term *nature* as indicating *capacity*. Thus the old nature of the flesh is that capactiy which all men have to serve and please Satan, sin, and self; whereas the new nature of the Spirit is that capacity to serve God, righteousness, and others.[16]

Sanctification may be viewed as involving vivification and mortification.

Sanctification, as a principle, is a holy, living principle, infused by regeneration. From this quickening (vivification) there flows forth a living by faith in Christ, walking in newness of life, living soberly, righteously, and godly.

Sanctification does not mean the abolition of the body of sin in regenerate and sanctified persons. Though the saints do not live in sin, it still lives in them, and sometimes it becomes very active and powerful. What is meant here (mortification) is the weakening of the power

---

15. John Gill, *A Body of Doctrinal Divinity* (Atlanta: Turner Lassetter, 1957), 552.
16. Charles C. Ryrie, *Balancing the Christian Life* (Chicago: Moody, 1969), 34 ff. See Appendix B for a discussion of Paul's account in Romans 7:14-25 of the conflict between these two natures.

of sin and a putting to death of the deeds of the body so that a course of sin is not persisted in. For this the Spirit of God and His grace are necessary (Rom. 8:13; Col. 3:5).

Sanctification may be viewed in its holy actings.

With respect to God, it consists in a holy reverence of Him—a godly fear. "The fear of the Lord is the beginning of knowledge" (Prov. 1:7, KJV).

It also includes love for Him. Jesus said to a lawyer, "You shall love the Lord your God with your whole heart, with your whole soul, and with your whole mind" (Matt. 22:37, *New Berkeley*). An unsanctified man cannot love the God who is pure and holy. The carnal mind is enmity to God. Note what Job says of the hypocrite: "Will he delight himself in the Almighty? Will he call upon God at all times?" (Job 27:10, *New Berkeley*).

It resides in joyful submission to the will of God in all things. Perhaps the *essence* of sanctification lies in the joyful conformity of our wills to the will of God. The writer of the epistle to the Hebrews concludes his epistle with the prayer that the God of peace may equip his readers "in every good thing to do His will" (Heb. 13:20-21, NASB).

It also lies in religious exercises and in acts of devotion to God. This means a faithful attendance on the mininstry of the Word and the administration of the sacraments; and in fervent prayer, which is the breath of a sanctified soul toward God. But it also means serving Him in the world. God is to be the rule and measure not only of our "religious" activities but of all the *actions* of our life. "Indeed, nothing more absurd can be imagined than wise, sublime, and heavenly prayers added to a life where neither labor nor diversions, neither time nor money, are under the direction of the wisdom and desires of our prayers."[17]

Sanctification also rests in the eager desire of the soul for communion with God. "Our fellowship is with the Father and with his Son Jesus Christ" (1 John 1:3, KJV).

In addition, it consists in seeking the glory of God in *all* one does. "So, whether you eat or drink or whatever you do, do it all to the glory of God" (1 Cor. 10:31, *Berkeley*). Those who make a show of their religion seek only their own glory and as a result sign the receipt of their reward in full (Matt. 6:1; see John 7:18).

---

17. William Law, *A Serious Call to a Devout and Holy Life* (Philadelphia: Westminster, 1955), 18.

With respect to Christ, sanctification consists in our continuing to subject ourselves to Him as our Lord. "Jesus said to his disciples: 'If anyone wants to follow in my footsteps he must give up all right to himself, take up his cross and follow me' " (Matt. 17:24, *Phillips*).[18]

It also rests in setting Him before us as our example. "Christ suffered for you and left you a personal example, and wants you to follow in his steps" (1 Pet. 2:21, *Phillips*).[19] We must constantly desire a greater conformity to His image. "Sanctified souls desire to be with Christ, that they might be perfectly like him, as well as see him as he is."[20]

Sanctification also rests in coming to Him for cleansing. "If we confess our sins, He is faithful and just to forgive us our sins and to cleanse us from all unrighteousness" (1 John 1:9, *New Berkeley.*)[21]

With respect to the Holy Spirit, sanctification consists in minding, relishing, the things of the Spirit. "For people who live by the standard set by their lower nature are usually thinking the things suggested by that nature, and people who live by the standard set by the Spirit are usually thinking the things suggested by the Spirit" (Rom. 8:5, *Williams*).

It also resides in walking after the leadings and teachings of the Spirit—"who do not walk according to the flesh, but according to the Spirit" (Rom. 8:4, NASB; cf. Gal. 5:5, 25; Rom. 12:11; 15:13).

It rests in carefulness not to grieve the Spirit by whom we have been sealed unto the day of redemption (Eph. 4:30).

It lies in carefulness not to quench the Spirit by whom spiritual gifts are exercised (1 Thess. 5:19). The word *quench* literally means "to extinguish" a flame (Mark 9:48), or lamp (Matt. 25:8); metaphorically it means "to suppress," "to stifle." The negative *not* is employed with the present imperative; hence, "Stop quenching the Spirit." Some of the Thessalonians were already quenching the Spirit by attempting to stifle the exercise of the special gifts which He had sovereignly bestowed upon them (1 Thess. 5:20). It would seem best on the basis of context to understand the primary reference to the extraordinary gifts of the Spirit rather than to His ethical fruits.

18. On the question, Must Christ be Lord to be Saviour? see Ryrie, pp. 169-81. For a fuller discussion of this point, see Dietrich Bonhoeffer, *The Cost of Discipleship* (New York: Macmillan, 1959).
19. On the imitation-of-Christ concept, see Helmut Thielicke, Theological Ethics, *Foundations,* vol. 1 (Philadelphia: Fortress, 1966), 185-94.
20. Gill, 555.
21. See further on this point John R. W. Stott, *Confess Your Sins* (Philadelphia: Westminster, 1964).

With respect to sin, sanctification includes a hatred of sin and lamentation over it. One who has the grace of holiness abhors himself for his sin. Paul cries out, "Wretched man that I am!" (Rom. 7:24*a*, KJV); cf. Ps. 119:113).

It consists in constant strenuous effort to abstain from sin. The grace of God implanted in the heart, as well as displayed in the Word, teaches us to deny ungodliness and worldly lusts (Titus 2:11-12).

It also takes in earnest desires to be wholly freed from sin. In the same verse as quoted above, the apostle also cries out, "Who shall deliver me from the body of this death?" (Rom. 7:24*b*, KJV).

With respect to others, sanctification consists in a manifestation of the fruit of the Spirit. "The fruit of the Spirit is love, joy, peace, long-suffering, kindness, goodness, faithfulness, meekness, self-control; against such there is no law" (Gal. 5:22-23, ASV). The word *fruit* as in contrast to *works* (v. 19) indicates clearly that the Christian cannot produce these virtues of himself—they must be wrought by the Spirit. Further, the singular stresses the fact that this work of the Spirit constitutes a unity. Let us briefly examine this fruit.

Love. According to the context this is to be understood as love especially for the brethren (cf. vv. 13-14). This is the root of all other virtues (1 Cor. 13:13). This love is outgoing action on the behalf of others which is unmotivated by a desire for personal enrichment or by the worth of the object being loved. Such love only the Spirit can produce![22]

Joy. This is "that spiritual gladness which acceptance with God and change of heart produce. . . . It is conscious elevation of character, the cessation of the conflict in its earlier stage (v. 16-17), the opening up of a new world, and the hope of final perfection and victory."[23] Joy is an inner stability of soul which transcends all outward circumstances. Happiness depends on happenings but joy depends on Jesus.

Peace. Fundamentally, this is peace *with* God; secondarily, it includes peace with oneself and his neighbor.

Long-suffering. This is patience; it is opposed to failure to control one's temper. It enables us to bear injury without seeking revenge.

Kindness. This means gentleness, affability, graciousness. It invovles giving a soft answer.

---

22. For a classic treatment on *love,* see Anders Nygren, *Agape and Eros* (New York: Harper Torchbooks, 1969).
23. John Eadie, *Commentary on the Epistle of Paul to the Galatians* (Grand Rapids: Zondervan, n.d.), 422.

Goodness. "It is difficult to distinguish it from the previous term. . . . It may signify beneficence . . . kindness in actual manifestation."[24]

Faithfulness. This is trustfulness toward God and man: "Confidence in God, in all His promises, and under all His dispensations; and a spirit of unsuspicious and generous confidence towards men—not moved by doubts and jealousies, nor conjuring up possible causes of distrust, and treasuring up sad lessons from previous instances of broken plight."[25]

Meekness. This means submissiveness to God and gentleness toward man. Meekness is not weakness but true strength of character.

Self-control. This means ability to bridle the passions and appetites. "The word is to be taken in its widest significance, and not principally in reference to sexual sin. . . . This virtue guards against all sins of personal excess and is specially opposed to drunkenness and revellings as works of the flesh."[26]

SUBJECTS OF SANCTIFICATION

The sanctified are the elect of God. All whom God chose in eternity, He sanctifies in time; those who are a chosen generation become a holy people. They are the redeemed ones. The subjects of election, redemption, and sanctification are the same persons. Those who are chosen by the Father, and redeemed by the Son, are sanctified by the Spirit (Isa. 62:12).

Sanctification involves the totality of the redeemed one's being—body, soul, and spirit (1 Thess. 5:23).

The soul and/or spirit. (1) The understanding is enlightened to discern holy and spiritual things. "And be renewed in the spirit of your mind" (Eph. 4:23, KJV). (2) The will is bowed to the will of God, to serve Him. "For it is God who is at work within you, giving you the will and the power to achieve his purpose" (Phil. 2:13, *Phillips*). (3) The affections are made holy. "In brotherly love be affectionate to one another" (Rom. 12:10, *Williams*).

The body, all its members. "Do not go on presenting the members of your body to sin as instruments of unrighteousness; but present yourselves to God . . . and your members as instruments of righteousness to God" (Rom. 6:12-13, NASB)

24. Ibid., 423.
25. Ibid., 424.
26. Ibid.

CAUSES OF SANCTIFICATION

The *efficient* cause is the triune God—the Father (1 Thess. 5:23; 1 Pet. 1:15-16; 5:10), the Son (Heb. 2:11), and the Holy Spirit (1 Pet. 1:2).

The *moving* cause is the good will of God (1 Thess. 4:3).

The *instrumental* cause is the Word and acts of God. In His great intercessory prayer, Jesus said, "Sanctify them in the truth; thy word is truth" (John 17:17, ASV). The Word is disclosed in three ways: (1) written—the Bible; (2) preached—the sermon; (3) symbolized—in the sacraments. The acts of God sometimes take the form of afflictions. "Now obviously no 'chastening' seems pleasant at the time: it is in fact most unpleasant. Yet when it is all over we can see that it has quietly produced the fruit of real goodness in the characters of those who have accepted it in the right spirit" (Heb. 12:11, *Phillips*; cf. Ps. 119:67, 71).

PROPERTIES OF SANCTIFICATION

Sanctification involves the believer being *positionally* set apart unto God by virtue of his new life in Christ. This is not a matter of the degree of one's spirituality. Concerning the carnal Christians at Corinth Paul wrote, "But ye were washed, but ye were sanctified, but ye were justified in the name of the Lord Jesus Christ, and in the Spirit of our God" (1 Cor. 6:11, ASV; the past tense of the Greek verbs point to these acts as already accomplished).

Sanctification includes the believer being *experientially* set apart unto God by virtue of the ministry of the indwelling Spirit.

The work of regeneration is instantaneous, consisting in one single creative act; hence, it is not subject to degrees. No one is more or less regenerate than another; one is either dead or alive. But sanctification is progressive and admits of degrees; one may be more sanctified than another.

Scripture frequently enjoins upon believers an increase and growth in holiness. The apostle Peter exhorts, "But grow in the grace and knowledge of our Lord and Saviour Jesus Christ" (2 Pet. 3:18, ASV). Paul states of the Thessalonians, "We ought always to give thanks to God for you, brethren, as is only fitting, because your faith is greatly enlarged, and the love of each one of you all toward one another grows ever greater" (2 Thess. 1:3, NASB). The Bible speaks of our *growing* in grace, *abounding* in hope and love, and *increasing* in the knowledge of divine things. There would be no occasion for such speaking if experiential sanctification were perfected at the moment of regeneration.

Sanctification also involves the believer's being *completely* set apart

unto God, in that ultimately his practice and position will be brought
into perfect accord (see Eph. 5:26-27; Jude 24-25).

We may diagrammatically represent these three aspects of sanctification as follows:

THE THREEFOLD ASPECT OF SANCTIFICATION		
Past	*Present*	*Future*
Positional standing	Experiential state	Complete state brought up to standing
Instantaneous gift 1 Cor. 6:11	Progressive task 1 Pet. 1:15-16	Climactic 1 John 3:2

Sanctification is commanded for every Christian, without distinction
(1 Thess. 4:3). It is not the responsibliity of an elite group within the
church. Unfortunately, we tend to adopt two standards of Christian
commitment, one for "full-time Christian workers" and another for
"Christian laymen." But Scripture speaks of *all* believers as saints
("holy ones," 1 Cor. 1:1-2).

The basis of the divine command to holiness of life is God's ethical
holiness. Because God is holy He commands His creatures to be holy
(1 Pet. 1:15-16; cf. Lev. 19:2).

In sanctification God fulfills His original creative purpose; that is,
the making of man after His own image (Gen. 1:26; cf. 2 Cor. 3:18).

Sanctification

Baxter, James Sidlow. *Christian Holiness Restudied and Restated.*
    Grand Rapids: Zondervan, 1977.

Berkouwer, G. C. *Faith and Sanctification.* Translated by John
    Vriend. Grand Rapids: Eerdmans, 1952.

Bloesch, Donald G. *The Crisis of Piety.* Grand Rapids: Eerdmans,
    1968.

Pentecost, J. Dwight. *Pattern for Maturity.* Chicago: Moody, 1966.

Prior, Kenneth Francis William. *The Way of Holiness: A Study in
    Christian Growth.* Rev. ed. Downers Grove, Ill.: Inter-Varsity, 1982.

Ryle, J. C. *Holiness, Its Nature, Hindrances, Difficulties, and Roots.*
    London: James Clarke, 1956.

Ryrie, Charles C. *Balancing the Christian Life.* Chicago: Moody, 1969.

6
The Assurance for Salvation

Perseverance does not mean that everyone who professes faith in Christ and who is accepted into a church is thereby secure for eternity. Many who profess to have salvation do not possess it. Neither does it mean that it is impossible for a Christian to backslide, that is, to move in a direction of disobedience to God for a time (cf. Luke 22:31-34).

Apostasy (falling away) does not denote a loss of salvation. Instead, it is a deliberate, decisive rejection of the gospel on the part of one who has known it but never committed himself to the Christ of whom it witnesses (2 Pet. 2:20-21; note the comments on Heb. 6, pp. 95-97 of this book.).

Professing Christians may come into such close contact with the supernatural forces of the gospel that they continue for some time to be scarcely distinguishable in their manner of life from those who are actual possessors of Christ's life. However, testing eventually proves their faith to be temporary (cf. Mark 4:2-9).

Perseverance is a much more adequate term than *eternal security* to describe the scriptural concept intended here. "It is utterly wrong to say that a believer is secure quite irrespective of his subsequent life of sin and unfaithfulness. The truth is that the faith of Jesus Christ is *always respective* of the life of holiness and fidelity."[1]

---

1. John Murray, *Redemption: Accomplished and Applied* (Grand Rapids: Eerdmans, 1955), 154.

Some prefer the term *preservation,* believing that it best indicates that it is God alone who carries out the saving purpose of His electing love.[2] Perhaps it would be well to utilize both terms for a more adquate definition of the concept.

The synthesis of the preservation of God and the perseverance of the saints is well expressed by Peter: "Who by the power of God are guarded through faith unto a salvation ready to be revealed in the last time" (1 Pet. 1:5, ASV). Note especially the following three things in this text.

1. Believers are *kept.* The term which Peter uses is a military one. It means that our life is garrisoned by God, that He stands over us all our days.

2. Believers are kept *through* faith. The final preservation of believers is never divorced from the use of means.

> The Scriptural truth of final preservation is not the doctrine that a man who has truly believed is secure of ultimate salvation without any regard to his behaviour; but, on the contrary, it is the doctrine that God secures the ultimate salvation of every true believer by effecting, through the power of the Holy Spirit, his free persistence in Christian faith and obedience to the very end.[3]

3. Believers are kept *unto* salvation. This undoubtedly refers to the final consummation, the salvation to be revealed in the last time (Rom. 13:11; Heb. 1:14; 9:28).

THREE HISTORICAL VIEWS REGARDING PERSEVERANCE
REMONSTRANTS

The Remonstrants—followers of Jacob Arminius and led by Bisschop and Grotius—presented to Holland and Friesland in 1610 a series of articles known as the Remonstrance. Among these articles was one which taught that true believers could and often did fall away, completely and finally, from saving faith. The heart of their opposition was found in their idea of freedom and the *tension* that this freedom would inevitably bring. It was objected that if believers are confident that their election is inalienable they would then lack in a sense of responsibility and of the seriousness of sin. The fact of the matter is that the Reformed position does not deny that believers offer resistance to God

---

2. Herman Kuiper, *By Grace Alone: A Study in Soteriology* (Grand Rapids: Eerdmans, 1955), 138.

3. Ernest F. Kevan, *Salvation* (Grand Rapids: Baker, 1963), 96.

and that this results in loss for them, but it does deny that this resistance can be total and final.

ROME

According to Catholic doctrine, grace can be lost. The sacraments communicate many graces but they do not establish a will that is irrevocably turned to God. Rome maintains that both Scripture and experience teach that in the midst of the Christian's warfare there is always the possibility of radical and total apostasy; saving grace can be lost. Penance is the sacrament Christ instituted primarily in connection with lapses from grace.

As one studies the position of the Remonstrants and Rome, he soon discovers that it is synergism which is at the heart of the opposition to the doctrine of the perseverance of the saints. (The term *synergism* means literally "working together"; the thought here is that in the work of individual salvation both man and God cooperate.)[4]

LUTHERANS

The controversy with the Lutherans was quite different from that with the Roman Catholics. Later, however, when synergism became an increasing part of Lutheran theology, the points of similarity greatly increased. Initially Lutherans rejected the doctrine of the perseverance of the saints, but they did not deny the assurance of salvation. In the case of the Remonstrants and Rome, both of these concepts were rejected.

Lutherans accused the Reformed position of developing the concept of perseverance and assurance a priori from election, of proceeding logically from the unchangeable decree of election to the inalienability of persevering grace. As Professor Berkouwer well states, this chart was not correct. "We can be all the more thankful to be able to establish that in the doctrine of the Reformed churches the assurance of salvation is not at all connected with or founded on abstract information about God's election. . . . They did not wish to deviate from Calvin's thought of Christ as the 'mirror of election.' "[5]

Gerhard maintains, with other Lutherans, that one must differentiate between *total* and *final* falling (cf. Ezek. 18:24). He exegetes 1 John

4. See Everett F. Harrison, ed., *Baker's Dictionary of Theology* (Grand Rapids: Eerdmans, 1960), 510
5. G. C. Berkouwer, *Faith and Perseverance,* Studies in Dogmatics, vol. 6 (Grand Rapids: Eerdmans, 1958), 60.

2:19 as teaching that the elect can fall totally for a time, but never *finally*. In this way he both affirmed the assurance of salvation and opposed the Reformed confession of perseverance.[6]

BIBLICAL SUPPORT
(This list of texts is selective, not exhaustive.)

JOHN 6:39-40

This is the will of Him who sent Me, that of all that He gave Me I shall lose nothing but shall raise it up at the last day. For this is My Father's will, that every one who sees the Son and believes in Him will have eternal life, and I shall raise him up at the last day (John 6:39-40, *New Berkeley*).

The doctrine of the perseverance of the saints is taught here in unmistakable terms. Christ Himself teaches us that the elect (those given by the Father to the Son, v. 37) will be kept (guarded) to the very end. "In the Divine decree all is fixed beyond the possibility of man's will to change. God has a will for men in the mission of His Son, and the Son has come to execute it; and whatever opposition the execution of it may meet with, all is definite and certain. There is nothing haphazard in this work. God has entrusted it to One who will lose nothing of it, but who will raise it all up at the last day."[7]

JOHN 10:27-30

My sheep listen to My call; I know them and they follow me. I give them eternal life and they will never perish, and no one will snatch them out of my hand. My Father, who gave them to Me, is greater than all and no one can wrest them out of My Father's hand. I and the Father are One (John 10:27-30, *New Berkeley*).

Three statements in this passage emphasize perseverance.

1. Christ has made certain ones His sheep by giving them *eternal life* (cf. 3:16; 10:10). This new life differs qualitatively from that which characterizes the present age, and quantitatively in that it will never end.

2. Christ states that such will *never perish*. They shall never enter again into a state of condemnation, the condition of being banished forever from the presence of God. The Greek text contains the emphatic double negative here!

---

6. Ibid., 68 ff.
7. George Reith, *The Gospel According to John,* Handbooks for Bible Classes and Private Students, vol., 1 (Edinburgh: T & T Clark, 1889), 105.

3. He asserts that no one shall snatch them out of either His hand or His Father's. "The greatness of the Father, not of the flock, is the ground of the safety of the flock."[8] Paul puts the same truth more lyrically in Romans 8:38-39.

JOHN 17:11; CF. 11:42

Holy Father, preserve in Thy name those whom Thou hast given Me, so that they may be one as We are (John 17:11, *New Berkeley*).
I know that Thou dost always hear me (John 11:42, *New Berkeley*).

Our great High Priest prays that the Father *stand guard* over those whom He has given Him, that they be not overcome of the evil one or evil (17:15). The oneness for which He prays is not that of external ecclesiastical merger nor of ontological (essential) oneness with the triune God; rather, it is an inner spiritual oneness of purpose to stand over against the world in an effort to redemptively reach it.

1 JOHN 3:9

No one who is born of God makes a practice of sinning, because the God-given life principle continues to live in him, and so he cannot practice sinning, because he is born of God (1 John 3:9, *Williams*).

The expression "because His seed abides in him" (NASB) is variously interpreted. Some would suggest that "His seed" is a collective noun for the children of God; thus, "for the offspring of God abide in Him" (RSV, marg.). Others would hold, and this seems more probable, that "His seed" means "God's nature" (RSV) or "the divine seed" (NEB*) and that "in him" refers to the child of God. If this latter sense is accepted, the implication would then be that the new nature received at the new birth remains and exerts a strong internal pressure toward holiness.

The analogy of birth is also significant in respect to perseverance. The same principle applies in the spiritual world as in the natural. A son may fight and rebel against his father; but however unfilial his behavior may be, his conduct never makes him someone less than a son.

1 JOHN 5:18

We know that no one who is born of God makes a practice of sinning, but

---

*New English Bible.

8. A. T. Robertson, *The Fourth Gospel—The Epistle to the Hebrews,* Word Pictures in the New Testament, vol. 5 (New York: Harper, 1932), 186.

the Son who was born of God continues to keep him, and the evil one cannot touch him (1 John 5:18, *Williams*).

The King James Version reads, "He that is begotten of God keepeth himself." The preferred reading, however, renders the phrase "He who was born of God keeps him" (NASB, RSV). In this latter translation the subject of the verb (viz., "He that is begotten of God") is Christ, not the Christian. The truth then is not that the Christian keeps himself but rather that Christ keeps him. It is only as the Son "keeps" the Christian that the Christian can hope to "keep" God's commandments (3:24; 5:3).

PHILIPPIANS 1:6

I am certain of this very thing, that He who began the good work in you will go on until the day of Jesus Christ to complete it (Phil. 1:6, *Williams*).

In connection with our earlier discussion of the meaning of the biblical concept of perseverance, it is helpful to note the context of this reference. The preceding verse speaks of *human perseverance*—*"Your partnership in the gospel"* (v. 5, KJV). This text (v. 6) speaks of *divine preservation*—"He who began the good work in you will go on until the day of Jesus Christ to complete it." A discussion of this matter which does not fully recognize both of these elements is unscriptural.

Paul teaches us that our persevering is ultimately dependent on His persevering grace! "So then, my beloved, even as ye have always obeyed, not as in my presence only, but now much more in my absence, work out your own salvaton with fear and trembling; for it is God who worketh in you both to will and to work, for his good pleasure" (2:12-13, ASV).

1 PETER 5:10

And after you have suffered for a little, the God of all grace, who called you to His eternal glory in Christ, will Himself perfect, confirm, strengthen and establish you (1 Pet. 5:10, NASB).

Four important truths are put forth in this text. First, our divine calling is *in* Christ. Next, this call is from the God *of* grace—literally, "of every grace."

Third, this call is *unto* His eternal glory, and to that end Christ Himself will "perfect, confirm, strengthen and establish" us. God can be counted on to complete His saving work. *Perfect* means "restore." (This word is used of mending nets in Mark 1:19. Cf. also 2 Tim. 3:17, RSV; Luke 6:40). *Confirm* can be translated "make steadfast." (This was the kind of ministry to which our Lord called Peter, Luke 22:32.) *Strengthen* could also be "equip for active service." (This is the only place in the New Testament where this word occurs.) *Establish*—this word is omitted in some ancient manuscripts.

And, fourth, this call will find its fulfillment *after* believers have suffered a little while.

BIBLICAL WARNINGS

If we are to take seriously those many passages which warn against apostasy, must we not acknowledge the possibility of a real falling away from faith?

Those who oppose the doctrine of perseverance call to our attention the many "if" passages of the Bible. Note just a few of these:

"If a man abide not in me, he is cast forth as a branch, and is withered" (John 15:6, ASV).

"If ye keep my commandments, ye shall abide in my love" (John 15:10, ASV).

"Ye are my friends, if ye do the things which I command you" (John 15:14, ASV).

"For so be that ye continue in the faith . . ." (Col. 1:23, ASV).

"For we are become partakers of Christ, if we hold fast the beginnings of our confidence firm unto the end" (Heb. 3:14, ASV).

In addition to those passages which speak conditionally, we have a number which explicitly warn against apostasy as a real threat and which also indicate the reality of very serious lapses. Warnings against apostasy are especially frequent in the epistle to the Hebrews (3:12-13; 12:25; etc.). Actual cases of apostasy would include Saul Hymeneus, Alexander, Philetus, and Demas. Paul speaks in his epistles to Timothy of "some [who] . . . have made shipwreck of their faith" (1 Tim. 1:19, *Williams*) or who have "gone astray from the truth" (2 Tim. 2:18, *New Berkeley*). These and other passages such as Hebrews 6:4-8 and 2 Peter 2:1 would seem so forceful that it might be argued the doctrine of perseverance is hopelessly doomed to wreck itself on them.

In attempting to answer this line of argument, it must be pointed out that the many passages which speak of conditionality and apostasy (feared and actual) do not exhaust the entire biblical description of the relation between God's grace and faith. We must relate these statements to the *total* context of Scripture. Berkouwer states, "The opponents of the doctrine of perseverance knew these passages, of course; but they always stress that the 'if,' the conditional, must always be understood in the text, even though it is not found there in so many words. Further, such 'unconditional' texts, they said, had to be understood within 'the entire' conditional context of the Scriptures."[9] One cannot help but ask at this point on what basis it is to be concluded that unconditional passages are to be interpreted in the light of conditional and not vice versa. One suspects that dogmatic rather than strictly exegetical considerations determine the matter.

Berkouwer continues,

> It is apparent, however, that the expedient forced the opponents of perseverance into a standpoint which badly damaged the sovereignty of grace. If anything is certain, it is this, that according to the Scriptures God's grace does not stop short at the limits of human freedom of choice. Whoever claims this is bound to see faith and grace as two mutually exclusive and mutually limiting elements in salvation, and he is bound to emerge with a doctrine of grace that is synergistic in principle.[10]

If we properly understand the biblical relationship of faith to grace, then we will realize that our persevering cannot be a factor independent of God's preserving us. God's grace insures our persevering—but this does not make it any less *our* persevering. It is noteworthy that when Jude exhorts us to keep ourselves in the love of God (v. 21), he concludes with a doxology for Him who is able to keep us from falling and who will present us without blemish before the presence of His glory (v. 24). The warning passages are *means* which God uses in our life to accomplish His purpose in grace. "The profundity of the doctrine of perseverance must be sought precisely in the fact that admonition is included in it and that at the same time, through faith, perseverance is confessed as a gift."[11]

One of the most difficult passages in the area of perseverance is Hebrews 6. There are three major views which may be noted. First, there is the *saved-lost theory,* which argues that a true believer can be lost through deliberate apostasy.[12] It should be carefully noted, however, that this passage indicates the impossibility of repentance following such apostasy. (Other passages which might be understood to support this theory would include Matt. 24:13; Mark 3:29; Luke 9:62; Heb. 10:26; 1 John 5:16.)

Second, there is the *hypothetical theory,* which maintains that the writer is dealing with suppositions and not with fact, in order that he

---

9. Berkouwer, 90.
10. Ibid., 90-91.
11. Ibid., 111.
12. Charles W. Carter, ed., *The Wesleyan Bible Commentary,* vol. 6 (Grand Rapids: Eerdmans, 1966), 83 ff.

may correct wrong ideas.[13] Although much may be said in support of this view, it does seem to unduly minimize the impact of the warning.

Third, there is the *non-Christian theory,* which holds that there is no indication of saving faith in the hearts of the persons being described.[14] The experiences mentioned describe how exceedingly close it is possible to come to being a Christian without truly being one. Specifically the arguments for this view in respect to the wording of the text are the following ones.

1. "They were enlightened" (v. 4*a*). Those described here have been decisively confronted with the light of the gospel. To reject it meant that life could never the same again. It is possible that the verb translated "enlightened" could refer to baptism.[15]

2. "They had tasted the heavenly gift" (v. 4*b*). Not only have they been confronted with the light of the gospel; they have also in a measure understood and relished the revelation of God's mercy. Perhaps as enlightenment may suggest baptism, so the tasting (experiencing) of the heavenly gift may suggest the Eucharist. Obviously it is possible for people who have experienced both of the sacraments to commit apostasy.

3. "They had become partakers of the Holy Spirit" (v. 4*c*). To "partake of the Holy Spirit" is to be a sharer of His gifts or influences. The point here seems to be that not only had those described been baptized and received the Eucharist, they had also experienced the laying on of hands.

> Early apostolic history has a record of one outstanding character who believed when he heard the gospel, was baptized, attached himself to the evangelist whose preaching had convinced him, and presumably-received the Spirit when apostolic hands were laid upon him—yet Simon-Magus was pronounced by Peter to be still "in the gall of bitterness and in the bond of iniquity" (Acts 8:9ff., 18 ff.), and showed himself in the following decades to be the most determined opponent of apostolic Christianity. If we ask in what sense a man like that could have partaken of the Holy Spirit, the words that follow here may point the way to an answer.[16]

4. "They had tasted the good word of God and the powers of the age to come" (v. 5). Those described here had partaken of the gifts or influences of the Spirit in connection with the proclamation of the gospel

---

13. W. H. Griffith Thomas, *Hebrews: A Devotional Commentary* (Grand Rapids: Eerdmans, 1961), 74.

14. F. F. Bruce, *The Epistle to the Hebrews,* The New International Commentary on the New Testament, ed. F. F. Bruce (Grand Rapids: Eerdmans, 1964), 118 ff.

15. Ibid., 120.

16. Ibid., 120-22.

and the miraculous gifts by which this early beginning of Christianity was characterized. "Simon Magus realized how good the word of God was when he heard it from Phillip's lips and he was amazed at the signs and great 'powers' that accompanied the proclamation and reception of the gospel."[17] Even unregenerate men partook of such miraculous power (Matt. 7:22-23).

The persons here described, then, were persons who not only enjoyed what has been termed the common influences of the Holy Spirit, but His miraculous gifts—who not only witnessed the effects of these gifts in others but were partakers of them themselves."[18]

This passage would thus appear to be teaching us that God will pardon all who truly repent, but that Scripture and experience alike suggest that it is tragically possible for individuals to arrive at a state of heart and life where they can no longer repent.

Perseverance (Security)

Berkouwer, G. C. *Faith and Perseverance*. Grand Rapids: Eerdmans, 1958.

Glaze, R. E., Jr. *No Easy Salvation, A Careful Examination of the Question of Apostasy in Hebrews*. Nashville: Broadman, 1966.

Gromacki, Robert Glenn. *Salvation Is Forever*. Chicago: Moody, 1973.

Marshall, I. Howard. *Kept by the Power of God: A Study of Perseverance and Falling Away*. 2d. ed. Minneapolis: Bethany Fellowship, 1974.

PRAYER AND PERSEVERANCE

THE PRAYERS OF BELIEVERS THEMSELVES

There is power in prayer; it elicits an answer (note James 5:16). James points to Elijah as an example of this power. The power, however, resides in God's mercy. "Prayer can have fire and power only if it comes eagerly to *Him* and looks for *everything* from Him in boundless confidence."[19] Because of the power and efficacy of prayer it is not surprising that there is also a great emphasis on *perseverance* and *continuity* in prayer (1 Thess. 5:17; cf. Col. 4:2). Whatever Paul precisely means by his instruction to "pray without ceasing," it was not antithetical to continuous labor (1 Cor. 15:10). The apostle certainly

---

17. Ibid.
18. John Brown, *An Exposition of Hebrews* (London: Banner of Truth, 1961), 287.
19. Berkouwer, 128.

did not advocate a prayer-mysticism which suppresses ordinary life pursuits. In his Thessalonian epistles he specifically warns against this. (See also Eph. 6:18; cf. 1:8; Rom. 12:12; Col. 1:9; 2 Tim. 1:3).

True prayer is offered in *faith* (James 5:15); it expects nothing from itself but everything from God. It is such that it assumes significance in perseverance. "Constancy in life is not deducible in a deterministic way; it must be seen in the living relation between prayer and faith."[20] Perseverance is closely connected with prayer and is inconceivable apart from it. We persevere only *through the exercise of faith and prayer*. Prayer is one of the divinely ordained *means* of bringing Christians to eternal glory (Eph. 3:14-21; 2 Thess. 3:1; 1 Tim. 2:1-2).

THE INTERCESSION OF CHRIST

We cannot speak correctly of perseverance if we do not take into account the fact of Christ's high priestly intercession. Paul speaks succinctly but significantly of this in his doxology in Romans 8:31-35. Note especially verse 34: "Who is he that condemneth? It is Christ Jesus that died, yea rather, that was raised from the dead, who is at the right hand of God, who also maketh intercession for us" (ASV). "All present and future tribulations, all threats and dangers are summarized; but they fall away, or rather they are covered over by the one great love."[21] Clearly there is an immediate connection between the intercession of Christ and the utter impossibility of anything separating us from the love of Christ.

Another important passage in respect to Christ's intercession on our behalf is Hebrews 7:25: "Hence also He is able to save forever those who draw near to God through Him, since He always lives to make intercession for them" (NASB). Our great High Priest ensures our never failing acceptance before God (cf. Isa. 53:12).

> The inference is inescapable that the intercession of Christ brings within its scope all that is necessary to salvation in the fullest extent of its consummation perfection. This is to say that the intercession covers the whole range of what is requisite to and of what is realized in the eschatological salvation. The intercession of Christ is interposed to meet every need of the believer. No grace bestowed, no blessing enjoyed, no benefit received can be removed from the scope of the intercession, and the intercession is the guarantee that every exigency will be met by its efficacy. The security of

20. Ibid., 131.
21. Ibid., 132.

salvation is bound up with his intercession and outside of his intercession we must say that there is no salvation.[22]

A careful study of John 17 will help us to understand more fully what is intended when our Lord is described in the Hebrews passage as making intercession for those who come to God through Him. Three additional ideas may be observed.

1. Jesus' intercession is always efficacious; it always accomplishes the purpose intended (John 11:42).

2. His intercession includes those who are still unbelievers but who are among the elect (John 17:20-21). In John 17:1-5, Jesus' petitions have peculiar reference to Himself; verses 6-20, to His disciples; and verses 21-26, to the whole church. In verse 20 the precise distinction made is between the eleven, on the one hand, and all those who *are* brought to genuine faith in Christ through their word, on the other. Some had already been brought into the fold, but down through the entire reach of the new age others would be converted through their word and the word of those to follow them. "The eye of Jesus scans the centuries, and presses to his loving heart *all* his true followers, *as if they had all been saved even at this very moment.*"[23]

3. His intercession is part of a total high priestly work which also includes propitiation. The intercession is based on the atonement (Rom. 8:34; Heb. 7:25-27). They are coextensive in their intent.

Finally, as a clear illustration of the importance of Christ's intercessory ministry in perseverance, we may consider the experience of Peter in those closing days of our Lord's earthly life. Peter had a wrong view of perseverance. He found the basis for his continuance in himself. He saw Christ treading the path of sorrows, and he placed Christ's life in the light of his own faith and love. No matter how difficult the road, he wanted Christ to know that he could be counted on for support. Peter would console his Master in the hour of frightful isolation; Christ could count on Peter to never forsake Him. Here is a self-confidence which is diametrically opposed to true confidence.

In sharp contrast to this kind of "perseverance" is the intercession of Christ.

---

22. John Murray, *The Heavenly Priestly Activity of Christ* (The Campbell Morgan Lectureship, June 18, 1958), London: Westminster Chapel, Buckingham Gate), 13.
23. William Hendriksen, *Exposition of the Gospel According to John,* New Testament Commentary, vol. 2 (Grand Rapids: Baker, 1954), 363.

We behold the image of the praying Christ confronting the spectre of Satan with his sieve. It is through His intercession that a very different kind of permanency appears: "I have prayed for you, that your faith fail not!" It is Christ Himself who brought Peter to his senses, when He turned about and looked at him after the crowing of the cock (Luke 22:61). Peter's fall was miserable. He, the one who had confessed Christ at Caesarea Philippi, was the very one who forsook Him in the darkest hour of His life. He made his contribution to the total forsakenness of the Man of Sorrows. Truly, it was not Peter's faith, love, and faithfulness that preserved him. His life was saved by the intercession of Christ, when he had centered his attention on his own life alone, when all his moorings were cast away by his oath, and when it appeared that only chaff remained from Satan's sifting of his life.[24]

THE INTERCESSION OF THE HOLY SPIRIT

In relating the intercession of the Spirit specifically to perseverance, we turn once again to that same chapter of Romans in which Paul speaks of the intercession of Christ. "He who searches the hearts knows what the mind of the Spirit is, because He intercedes for the saints according to the will of God" (Rom. 8:27, NASB). In this statement the apostle teaches us that the Spirit compensates for what is lacking in our prayers. We are given insight here in respect to the relation between perseverance, the believer's weakness, and the assistance of the Holy Spirit. We are not left to ourselves in prayer; in our weaknesses the Holy Spirit takes up our case with the Father, with groanings that cannot be uttered. Incidentally but significantly, the praying referred to in this text is probably not that of the Spirit working in and through the prayers of the saints but rather a praying which the Spirit does Himself. Even though our prayers are dreadfully weak at their best, the Spirit's intervention brings a great consolation. Ultimate victory, perseverance in hope (Rom. 8:23-26), is only possible because of the Spirit's prayers which transcend our weaknesses. When we face the dangers, temptations, and trials of life we must realize, as Peter did, that we shall be preserved by the powerful intercession of Christ and His Spirit and that *ultimately* for that reason alone our faith did not die.

---

24. Berkouwer, 145.

7
The Climax of Salvation

GLORIFICATION is the final climactic act in God's redeeming work (Rom. 8:30). "Glorification is an event which will affect all the people of God together at the same point of time in the realization of God's redemptive purpose. It will bring to final fruition the purpose and grace which was given in Christ Jesus before times eternal (cf. 2 Tim. 1:9)."[1] God has purposed to complete His salvation with glory. "The finished work of creation was good but the completed work of redemption shall be glorious!"[2]

BASIS OF GLORIFICATION

As with all the preceding works, Christ is the sure foundation. "For no other foundation can any one lay than that which is laid, which is Jesus Christ" (1 Cor. 3:11, ASV).

Our eventual glorification is insured by Christ's death, resurrection, and intercession.

1. Christ's death—the final effective resolution of the problems

---

1. John Murray, *Redemption: Accomplished and Applied* (Grand Rapids: Eerdmans, 1955), 177.
2. Bernard Ramm, *Them He Glorified: A Systematic Study of the Doctrine of Glorification* (Grand Rap;ids: Eerdmans, 1963), 57.

created by man's sin. His death established the righteousness of God
(Rom. 3:25); effected reconciliation (2 Cor. 5:18-21); accomplished a
purification of sins (Heb. 1:3); and achieved redemption (Eph. 1:7).

2. Christ's resurrection—the vindication of God's satisfaction with
His Son's work.

3. Christ's intercession—the preservation of God's people, from the
moment of their calling until their glorification (Heb. 9:28; see also pp.
97-100, this book).

ASSURANCE OF GLORIFICATION

While the certainty of our glorification is grounded in the objective
work of Christ in history, our assurance respecting this fact is grounded
in certain factors arising out of the work of Christ as applied to
believers.

1. Our salvation is called a *promise* (Titus 1:2; 1 John 2:25). The concept of promise looks forward to a future fulfillment (Eph. 1:13; Heb.
11:13, 39; James 2:5; 2 Pet. 1:4).

2. Christ is the *firstfruits* of our salvation (1 Cor. 15:20, 23); so also is
the Holy Spirit (Rom. 8:23). Firstfruits are but the beginning of that
which shall eventually become a great harvest.

3. The Holy Spirit is the *earnest* of our salvation, our inheritance
(2 Cor. 1:22; 5:5; Eph. 1:14). An earnest is a down payment, a first in-
stallment, a pledge or guarantee of an eventual final payment and total
possession.

4. Our salvation is *sealed* (2 Cor. 1:22; Eph. 1:13; 4:30). The seal
marks ownership, quality, security. Again we should clearly understand
that it is the Spirit Himself who seals us unto the final day of redemption.

5. Our salvation is called an *inheritance* (Eph. 1:14, 18; 5:5; Col.
3:24; Heb. 9:15; 1 Pet. 1:3-4). This is clearly something in the future,
which shall be delivered at the set time of inheritance.

These five biblical terms describe our salvation as eschatological in
character. Our present redeemed state is only a beginning of what will
be accomplished in the age to come. Our glorification will occur at the
return of Christ.

Ramm correctly notes that

> the individual acts of our now-salvation are eschatological in character.
> Justification is eschatological in that it anticipates the complete vindication
> of the believer in the end-time (Rom. 5:9-10). Regeneration is eschato-
> logical in that it anticipates the time when all things shall be made new . . .
> Sanctification is eschatological in that it looks forward to the perfection of

all things. That which sums up the eschatological realization and fulfillment of our justification, our regeneration, and our sanctification is our
end-time glorification.[3]

NATURE OF GLORIFICATION

Glorification involves the perfecting of the *soul*.

While the New Testament represents our glorification as a complete
juridical exoneration, it also (and perhaps more frequently) views it as a
moral perfection. Note some of the specific terms employed.

Amōmos. This word was used in the Septuagint to indicate the
absence of defects in sacrificial animals (Num. 6:14; 19:2; etc.)—un-
blemished. In a moral or religious sense it means blameless. In Ephesians 5:27 Paul indicates that when the church is glorified by God, it
will be without moral blemish or spot: "So that He may present the
church to Himself gloriously, having no spot or wrinkle or any of such
thing, but holy and blameless" (*New Berkeley;* see also Eph. 1:4; Col.
1:22; Jude 24). Glorification coincides with ultimate sanctification.

Hagios. This term means holy, morally perfect. "You . . . He has
now reconciled in His human body through His death, to introduce you
into His presence holy and blameless and irreproachable" (Col. 1:22,
New Berkeley). No unholy person may ever enter heaven; only the holy
can endure and be with God in eternity. Our glorification then involves
our being rendered holy in Christ to the degree that we perfectly satisfy
the holiness of God.

Aproskopos. This denotes an absence of offensiveness; it means to
be free from cause of stumbling. Paul prays that the Philippians would
"be able always to recognize the highest and the best, and . . . live
sincere and blameless lives unto the day of Christ" (Phil. 1:10,
Phillips). The idea is "that of arriving at one's destination not *stumbled
against*, i.e., *uninjured* by any obstacles in the roads; hence, morally
uninjured, and so, *not worthy of blame, blameless.*"[4]

Elikrinēs. The image behind this word, coupled with *aproskepos*
(Phil. 1:10—see above) is that of something being tested by the sun,
hence, pure, unmixed, without spot, immaculate—"and may be pure."
"In the day of Christ believers shall be tested by the sunlight and not be
found wanting. Their glorification shall bestow upon them an immaculate purity which shall stand up under the eyes of him whose eyes

---

3. Ibid., 61.
4. William Hendriksen, *Philippians,* New Testament Commentary (Grand Rapids:
Baker, 1962), 61.

burn like a flame of fire (Cf. Rev. 1:4; 2:18; 19:12)."[5]

Anegklētos. This word means irreproachable, to be free from an incriminating charge. Paul used the term in 1 Corinthians 1:8 in reference to the final day: "Who shall also confirm you to the end, blameless in the day of our Lord Jesus Christ" (NASB). In that day Christians will stand before God completely free from all moral objections.

Amemptos. This term means faultless, blameless. In 1 Thessalonians 3:13 and 5:23 the word has eschatological meaning. According to the first passage, our hearts are to be strengthened so that they may be without fault in the presence of the Father at the return of Christ. In the second, the apostle indicates that the present process of sanctification will climax in our whole person—spirit, soul, and body—being blameless at the coming of our Lord Jesus Christ.

Spilos and *rhutis.* In Ephesians 5:25-27 Paul teaches us that the church (viewed corporately) will be free from all moral spots and wrinkles in the end-time.

Glorification also involves full participation in eternal life. The important word here is *full* participation. God's grace in Christ brings believers even now into eternal life (John 5:24); but the *fullness* of this life is yet to be realized (vv. 25-28).

Eternal life includes two ideas—a new quality of life and a never ending life. When the sinner is restored to his proper relationship with God through Christ he enters a new life—a life in harmony with the life of God Himself. This is a kind of life infinitely superior to that life previously possessed; it is indeed an abundant life. Glorification means the full bestowal of eternal life upon believers—a perfect relationship with God that has a sublime quality about it and which is of eternal duration.

Glorification also includes the full realization of freedom. This may be viewed in three respects: freedom from sin, from the law, and from death.

Freedom from sin (John 8:33-36; Rom. 6-8; Gal. 5:1, 13) is partial now but will be complete at the coming of Christ. We still have the fallen nature; then, it will be utterly done away with. At that time we will have the freedom to do only the good.

The Christian is free from the law both with respect to justification and to sanctification. These concepts are clearly described by Paul in Romans and Galatians.

However, it would seem reasonable to suggest that although the

5. Ramm, 71.

moral law of God presently provides guidelines for the conduct of believers, in the future age the necessity of such law will no longer exist—the saints shall have been glorified (Matt. 5:17-18). The law is the mediator of God's will for fallen creatures.

Death is the wages of sin; although the Christian is not exempt from the experience of dying, he is exempt from its sting (1 Cor. 15:56). Because of the death and resurrection of Christ, the Christian need not fear this king of terrors (Heb. 2:14-18).

Thus we learn that the complete realization of our freedom in Christ is to be enjoyed at our glorification (Rom. 8:18-25; 2 Cor. 4:16-18). Then we shall be what we truly are. While in this life we strive to be like our Lord; then, our souls shall be perfectly conformed to His image (Rom. 8:28-29). "Glorification is . . . the perfecting of our manhood into the image of the perfect human nature of Jesus Christ."[6]

Glorification also incorporates the perfecting of the *body*. The concept of glorification must be understood as involving the total man—soul and/or spirit together with the body.

The Bible attributes a real dignity to the human body. (1) Note the *total* man is in the image of God (Gen. 1:26-30; 2:4-8, 15-18). (2) The Genesis account teaches us that man is not a soul merely inhabiting a body but rather an ensouled body (2:7). Man is a psycho-physical unity. (3) Man with his body is included under the divine pronouncement that all things are good (Gen. 1:31). (4) The focal point of divine judgment is death. Although the decease of the body does not exhaust the biblical concept of death, it is nevertheless central to it. Physical death is the outward sign of spiritual death.

Christ's resurrection guarantees ours. (1) Christ rose from the dead in a substantial body (Matt. 28:9; Luke 24:39, 43, 50; John 20:17, 22, 27). (2) His body was of the new age, glorious, and is the pattern after which ours will be fashioned (Phil. 3:20-21; cf. 2 Cor. 5:1-5).

The King James Version renders Philippians 3:21: "Who shall change our vile body . . . " The word *vile* should be rendered "lowly" (*Williams,* RSV). Although many Greek pagans viewed the body as the prison of the soul, Paul viewed the body as ideally fashioned for the abode of the Holy Spirit (1 Cor. 6:19). To be sure, presently, because of the influence of sin, it is "the body of our *humiliation*." In this condition it is subject to sin's curse—weakness, suffering, sickness, and death—but at Christ's return it will be refashioned after the glorious

---

6. Ibid., 90.

body of our Lord (1 John 3:2). The nature of this great change is outlined in some detail in 1 Corinthians 15.

Glorification

Hoyt, Herman A. *The End Times*. Chicago: Moody, 1969.

Manley, George T. *The Return of Jesus Christ*. Chicago: Inter-Varsity, 1960.

Pache, Rene. *The Future Life*. Translated by Helen I. Needham. Chicago: Moody, 1962.

Ramm, Bernard. *Them He Glorified: A Systematic Study of the Doctrine of Glorification*. Grand Rapids: Eerdmans, 1963.

Smith, Wilbur M. *The Biblical Doctrine of Heaven*. Chicago: Moody, 1980.

Appendix A

THE ORDO SALUTIS

THE *ordo salutis* (the way of salvation) has to do with the process whereby the work of salvation, accomplished in Christ, is subjectively realized in the hearts of men. It has to do with the application of the objective work of Christ in the believer. It views the matter of application in terms of a logical order, not in terms of the temporal sequence. The emphasis is not on what man does in appropriating the grace of God but on what God does in applying it. Berkhof states,

> When we speak of an *ordo salutis,* we do not forget that the work of applying the grace of God to the individual sinner is a unitary process, but simply stress the fact that various movements can be distinguished in the process, that the work of application of redemption proceeds in a definite and reasonable order, and that God does not impart the fulness of His salvation to the sinner in a single act.[1]

THREE MAJOR VIEWS

LUTHERAN

Evangelical Lutherans view the *ordo salutis* as the subjective realization of the divine redemptive work of Christ; however, they emphasize

---

1. L. Berkhof, *Systematic Theology* (Grand Rapids: Eerdmans, 1941), 416.

what is done on the part of man rather than what is done on the part of God. In general, their construction of the *ordo salutis* is as follows:

Calling. In Christ, God is reconciled to the world of humanity. God proclaims this fact to man in the gospel, and He offers to put man in possession of that forgiveness and righteous standing historically accomplished in Christ. This call to salvation always brings a certain measure of saving grace to all who hear the Word, a grace which enables the sinner to respond to the message but a grace which also may be resisted.

Illumination. The call of God is always accompanied with a certain measure of illumination and quickening so that one may understand both the wrath and the grace of God.

Conversion (repentance). If the grace of God contained in the word of the gospel is not resisted, it frequently results in repentance and conversion.

Regeneration. Conversion may issue in regeneration (new birth) by which the Holy Spirit grants faith in the gospel.

Justification. The four preceding steps (calling, illumination, conversion, regeneration) are a preparatory process. When there is faith, justification follows immediately. It involves the forgiveness of sins and the title to eternal life on the basis of the righteousness of Christ embraced by faith.

Mystical union. This saving faith also brings mystical union with Christ.

Renovation. This is the power to promote one's process of sanctification. Good works necessarily result from a living faith in Christ.

Conservation. The permanent possession of these blessings is conditioned by the continued exercise of faith on the part of man. If he ceases to exercise faith, a man may lose his salvation.

ARMINIAN

In general the Arminian distinctive contribution in the construction of an *ordo salutis* is as follows:

External call. The external call of the gospel is accompanied by a universal sufficient grace which can however be resisted. This is "prevenient" grace.[2]

Repentance and faith. These two conscious responses of man precede regeneration (new birth). Although some Calvinists (including Calvin

---

2. Les G. Cox, "Prevenient Grace—A Wesleyan View," *Journal of the Evangelical Theological Society,* vol. 12, pt. 3 (Summer 1969): 143 ff.

himself) state this, they do so in an ultimately different sense. In the Arminian view, the human will is considered to be one of the *causes* of regeneration. This position is clearly synergistic.

Sanctification. The believer is able, in sanctification, to attain in this life a state of perfection—perfect love.

Perseverance. As long as a believer lives he may fall away from grace so as to lose his salvation.

REFORMED

In general the Reformed construction of the *ordo salutis* is as follows:

Calling. This is general and effectual.

Regeneration. It is the implantation of the principle of life by the Spirit in the heart of the elect. (A. Kuyper reverses *calling* and *regeneration.*)

Conversion. This is repentance and faith.

Justification. It is the constitutive and declarative act whereby sinners are reckoned righteous.

Sanctification. This is the progressive growth in holiness of life; a renewal after the image of Christ.

Perseverance. This is the eternal preservation of the saints through the faithfulness of God.

Glorification. This is the final redemption of the saints in the totality of their being—body, soul, and/or spirit.

A DISCUSSION OF THE VALIDITY OF SUCH SCHEMES

The significant question is simply, Does the Bible supply information sufficient for the construction of a single fixed *ordo salutis*? In answer to this question John Murray states,

> God is not the author of confusion and therefore he is the author of order. There are good and conclusive reasons for thinking that the various actions of the application of redemption . . . take place in a certain order, and that the order has been established by divine appointment, wisdom and grace.[3]

Murray endeavors to support this thesis from various passages of Scripture. In John 3, Jesus told Nicodemus that unless one be born anew (or from above) and be born of water and the Spirit, he cannot see the kingdom of God. From this passage it is clear that there is an order,

---

3. John Murray, *Redemption: Accomplished and Applied* (Grand Rapids: Eerdmans, 1955), 98.

that is, new birth precedes entrance into the kingdom.

In 1 John 3:9 the apostle deals with deliverance from the reigning power of sin. "No one who is born of God makes a practice of sinning, because the God-given life principle continues to live in him, and so he cannot practice sinning, because he is born of God" (*Williams*). This text indicates that the reason a person is delivered from the reigning power of sin is that he is born of God, and the reason he continues in his freedom from the power of sin is that the seed (nature) of God abides in him. The new birth, therefore, is prior to freedom from sin (cf. 1 John 5:16).

In John 1:12, faith is prior to adoption; in Ephesians 1:13, hearing and believing are prior to sealing of the Spirit.

From such texts Murray concludes, "These texts prove the fact of order and show that it is not empty logic to affirm divine order in the application of redemption."[4]

We must understand, however, that although these Scripture passages establish a logical priority of faith over various divine acts. they do not set out an order with respect to these separate concepts—regeneration (new birth), entrance into the kingdom, freedom from sins, sonship, sealing, and so forth.

Murray appeals to Romans 8:28-30 as a strong indication for an *ordo salutis*. In this passage the order is calling, justification, and glorification. There are so many intimations of order in this passage that we cannot but conclude that logical order of sequence is intended throughout. Note: (1) verse 28—God's purpose is prior to His calling; (2) verse 29—the progression of thought here is foreknowledge, then predestination; (3) verses 28-30—we cannot reverse foreknowledge and glorification; foreknowledge is the ultimate cause and glorification the ultimate end; (4) verse 30—foreknowledge and predestination are prior to calling, justification, and glorification; the reverse is inconceivable; and (5) verse 30—glorification cannot be prior to calling and justification.

Thus Murray argues that Romans 8:30 provides us with a *broad* outline of the logical order in the application of redemption.

From a different perspective, G. C. Berkouwer answers our question by asserting that there is a danger here of our failing to see the real motivation and purpose of the *ordo salutis* as expressed in the period of the Reformation. The Reformation emphasis was especially on the divine objective act of salvation rather than the human subjective response to it.

4. Ibid., 100.

A neatly systematized scheme of salvation is not an end in itself. The purpose of such is simply to aid us to appreciate the fullness of divine salvation; an *ordo salutis* is only valuable when it helps us to understand more clearly the message and reality of salvation. Berkouwer states, "The ways along which God leads man to His salvation are so richly varied that it is impossible to circumscribe them all in fixed stadia."[5]

From the biblical perspective Berkouwer significantly points out that if Paul had intended in Romans 8 to construct a complete, fixed *ordo salutis* he certainly would not have omitted sanctification from his list. In this passage Paul

> evidently means to characterize salvation in Christ, the salvation which arises from the depths of the Father's heart and reaches out into time with an eternal blessing. The context suggests that Paul does not have a sequence in mind. He is talking about the work, and particularly the prayer of the Holy Ghost (Rom. 8:23, 26, 27), about hope (Rom. 8:24, 25), about love to God (Rom. 8:28), and about the cooperation of all things for the good of those who love Him (Rom. 8:28). A simple biblicism, which sees a sequence here, would bring us into trouble when faced with 1 Corinthians 6:11, which puts sanctification before justification.[6]

In Berkouwer's opinion any theological study of the way of salvation must revolve around the correlation between faith and justification. He states,

> It must simply cut away everything which blocks its perspective of this *sola fide*. Heresy always invades the *ordo salutis* at this point, and this is why it is so necessary to realize that the entire *way of salvation* is only meant to illuminate *sola fide* and *sola gratia*. For only thus can it be confessed that *Christ is the way*.[7]

The Reformation spoke more simply and scripturally when it viewed the way of salvation in terms of the single correlation of grace and faith. In the *Institutes* Calvin's treatment of the *ordo salutis* continually centers on one point—salvation in Christ.[8] Berkouwer states,

---

5. G. C. Berkouwer, *Faith and Justification,* Studies in Dogmatics, vol. 3 (Grand Rapids: Eerdmans, 1962), 26.
6. Ibid., 31-32.
7. Ibid., 33.
8. See John Calvin, *Institutes of the Christian Religion,* Library of Christian Classics, vol. 20, ed. John T. McNeill and Henry P. Van Deusen (Philadelophia: Westminister, 1960), 3:1-4.

It would be unreasonable to criticize Calvin's method as being un-systematic. Though one does not find an *ordo salutis* in Calvin, in the sense of its later development, there is nonetheless an order, perhaps better called an orderliness, which is determined by salvation in Christ. Salvation in Christ—this is the center from which the lines are drawn to every point of the *way of salvation*. The lines themselves may be called faith. They connect every step on the way of salvation to salvation in Christ. Thus seen, the relation between the *way of salvation* and Christ's salvation will keep us from placing the objective and subjective elements of salvation opposite each other as a duality. The character of faith resolves all tension between objectivity and subjectivity. For faith has significance only in its orientation to its object—the grace of God. Thus, *sola fide,* instead of directing our attention to the believer, points us away from him to grace and God. We may apply this as a touchstone to every consideration of the *ordo salultis:* all lines of the life of faith must meet at the center, the grace of God.[9]

CONCLUSION

In conclusion the following points would seem to derive from our study.

1. Scripture does not provide us with a fixed or complete *ordo salutis.*

2. It would seem to allow for the legitimacy of constructing such for dogmatic or systematic reasons.

3. In this connection we gain some insight for our arrangement of topics from the Scriptures themselves, though we must use great caution here.

9. Berkouwer, 29.

Appendix B

ROMANS 7:14-25

A CRUCIAL QUESTION in this passage—Romans 7:14-25—concerns the nature of Paul's experience. Does he express himself as in a preconverted or converted state? Is there perhaps some better approach to the whole problem than that traditionally suggested?

In examining the issue certain things should be noted.

1. The section beginning with verse 14 has a change in the tense of the verbs. In the previous paragraph (vv. 7-13) the verbs are predominantly in the past tense (aorist), whereas from verse 14 onward they are in the present. This would seem to suggest that in the latter section Paul is writing of his present experience.

2. This latter paragraph also reflects a change in situation from that described in the immediately preceding section. In verses 7-11 the apostle describes himself as one who had been slain by the law; in verses 14-25 he speaks as an active combatant.

Richard N. Longenecker, apparently not noting these two factors, argues that "Romans 7:7-25 is not specifically either Paul's or mankind's preconversion state or postconversion experience. Nor is it the cry of only 'the man under the law' or 'the Christian who slips back into a legalistic attitude to God.' It is Paul uttering mankind's great cry of its own inability. It is Paul's and humanity's realization that in our history and experience we have become so bound up by sin that there can be deliverance and victory only through God."[1]

---

1. Richard N. Longenecker, *Paul: Apostle of Liberty* l(New York: Harper & Row, 1964), 114.

107

Longenecker is further not strictly accurate when he states concerning verse 25*b* that "the postconversion advocates either transpose the verse to an earlier position or omit any serious consideration of it."[2] Note for example the comments of John R. W. Stott: "Those who believe that God's purpose for us is to exchange the conflict of Romans 7 for the victory of Romans 8 must find the last sentence of chapter 7 a big stumbling-block, for immediately after the cry of exultant thanksgiving Paul reverts to the conflict and concludes with a summary of it: 'So then, I of myself serve the law of God with my mind, but with my flesh I serve the law of sin.' "[3] Concurring in this view is John Murray, who states, "In the latter part of verse 25 the apostle gives us in summary a reiteration of the life of conflict and contradiction which had been unfolded in detail in verses 14-24. This repetition would indicate that the triumphant thanksgiving in the early part of the verse does not itself bring to an end the conflict delineated."[4]

The two following arguments would seem to support the view that Paul is speaking of the conflict of the regenerate man in verses 14-25.

1. *Paul's view of himself* reflects only the thinking of a Christian. Verse 18: "For I know that nothing good has its home in me; that is, in my lower self" (*Williams*). Verse 24: "Wretched man that I am!" (KJV). The unbeliever is self-righteous: he would never acknowledge himself as a "wretched man"—in the sense in which Paul states this. Stott rightly observes, "Only the mature believer reaches the place both of self-disgust and of self-despair. It is he who recognizes with limpid clarity that in his flesh dwells nothing good. It is he who acknowledges his wretchedness and appeals with faith for deliverance."[5]

2. *Paul's opinion of the law* is decidedly Christian. He calls God's law "good" (v., 16); he expresses his desire to obey it (v. 22)—"For I delight in the law of God after the inward man" (ASV). What unregenerate man would say this? the attitude of the unbeliever toward the law is stated in 8:7: "Fleshly-mindedness is hostile to God;' it is not submissive to God's Law, in fact it cannot be" (*New Berkeley*). Paul states in 7:22 not that he is hostile to God's law but that he actually loves it!

---

2. Ibid., 111.
3. John R. W. Stott, *Men Made New: An Exposition of Romans 5-8* (Chicago: Inter-Varsity, 1966), 78.
4. John Murray, *The Epistle to the Romans,* New International Commentary on the New Testament, vol. 1, ed. Ned B. Stonehouse (Grand Rapids: Eerdmans, 1959), 270.
5. Stott, 73.

It would thus seem best to view this passage as descriptive of the conflict of the Christian, a conflict to which Christ is the answer.[6]

---

6. Note Paul Tournier, *Guilt and Grace* (New York: Harper & Row, 1962), 158 ff.

Helpful Books on Salvation

GENERAL WORKS

Arminius, James. *The Works of James Arminius*. 3 vols. Grand Rapids: Baker, 1956.

Aulén, Gustaf. *The Faith of the Christian Church*. Philadelphia: Muhlenberg, 1948.

Barth, Karl. *Church Dogmatics*. 10 vols. New York: Scribner, n.d.

Berkhof, L. *Systematic Theology*. Grand Rapids: Eerdmans, 1939.

Berkouwer, G. C. *Studies in Dogmatics*. 10 vols. Grand Rapids: Eerdmans, n.d.

Brunner, H. Emil. *Dogmatics*. 3 vols. Philadelphia: Westminster, 1950-62.

Buswell, J. Oliver. *A Systematic Theology of the Christian Religion*. Grand Rapids: Zondervan, 1967.

Calvin, John. *The Institutes of the Christian Religion*. 2 vols. Edited by John T. McNeill. Philadelphia: Westminster, 1960.

Chafer, Lewis Sperry. *Systematic Theology*. 8 vols. Dallas: Dallas Theo. Sem., 1948.

Colquhoun, John. *Repentance*. London: Banner of Truth, 1826.

Cullmann, Oscar. *Salvation in History*. New York: Harper & Row, 1967.

DeWolf, Harold L. *A Theology of the Living Church*. New York: Harper & Row, 1953.

Ebeling, Gerhard. *The Nature of Faith*. Translated by Ronald G. Smith. Philadelphia: Fortress, 1962.

Finney, Charles G. *Lectures on Systematic Theology*. South Gate, Cal.: Colporter Kemp, 1878; Grand Rapids: Eerdmans, 1951.

Gill, John. *Body of Divinity*. Atlanta: Turner Lassetter, 1839; Neptune, N. J.: Loizeaux, n.d.

Green, Michael B. *The Meaning of Salvation*. Philadelphia: Westminster, 1965.

Hammond, T. C. *In Understanding Be Men*. Chicago: Inter-Varsity, 1936.

Hodge, Charles. *Systematic Theology*. 3 vols. Grand Rapids: Eerdmans, 1946.

Hoeksema, Herman. *Reformed Dogmatics*. Grand Rapids: Reformed Free, 1966.

Hughes, Philip E. *But for the Grace of God*. Philadelphia: Westminster, 1964.

Johnson, E. Ashby. *Saved—from What?* Richmond: Knox, 1966.

Jones, E. Stanley. *Conversion*. New York: Abingdon, 1959.

Kevan, Ernest F. *Salvation*. Grand Rapids: Baker, 1963.

Knight, George A. F. *Law and Grace*. London: SCM Press, 1962.
Kung, Hans. *Justification*. New York: Nelson, 1964.
Kuitert, H. M. *The Reality of Faith*. Grand Rapids: Eerdmans, 1968.
Kuyper, Abraham. *Principles of Sacred Theology*. Grand Rapids: Eerdmans, 1954.
Lightner, Robert. *The Death That Christ Died: A Case for Unlimited Atonement*. Des Plaines, Ill: Reg. Bapt. 1967.
Litton, E. Arthur. *Introduction to Dogmatic Theology*. London: James Clarke, 1960.
Machen, J. Gresham. *What Is Faith?* Grand Rapids: Eerdmans, 1925.
Macquarrie, John. *Principles of Christian Theology*. New York: Scribner, 1966.
Marshall, Walter. *The Gospel—Mystery of Sanctification*. Grand Rapids: Zondervan, 1954.
Mikolaski, Samuel J. *The Grace of God*. Grand Rapids: Eerdmans, 1966.
Morris, Leon. *The Apostolic Preaching of the Cross*. Grand Rapids: Eerdmans, 1956.
Moule, H. C. G. *Christ and Sanctification*. London: Pickering & Inglis, n.d.
Murray, John. *Redemption: Accomplished and Applied*. Grand Rapids: Eerdmans, 1955.
Owen, John. *The Death of Death in the Death of Christ*. London: Banner of Truth, n.d.
Pieper, Francis. *Christian Dogmatics*. 4 vols. St. Louis: Concordia, 1950.
Prior, K. F. W. *Christian Doctrine of Sanctification, the Way of Holiness*. Chicago: Inter-Varsity, 1967.
Shedd, W. G. *Dogmatic Theology*. 3 vols. Grand Rapids: Zondervan, n.d.
Strong, A Hopkins. *Systematic Theology*. Philadelphia: Judson, 1907.
Thomas, W. H. Griffith. *The Principles of Theology*. London: Church Bk. Rm. Press, 1956.
Tillich, Paul. *Systematic Theology*. Chicago: U. of Chicago Press, n.d.
Whale, J. S. *Christian Doctrine*. New York: Cambridge U. Press, 1941.
Wiley, H. O. *Christian Theology*. 3 vols. Kansas City, Mo.: Nazarene Pub. House, 1940.

SOTERIOLOGY

Aulen, Christus. Gustaf. *Christus Victor: An Historical Study of the Three Main Types of the Idea of Atonement*. Translated by A. G. Herbert. New York: Macmillan, n.d.
Barclay, W. *Turning to God*. London:' Epworth, 1963.
Bloesch, S. Donald G. *The Crisis of Piety*. Grand Rapids: Eerdmans, 1968.
Bolton, Samuel. *The True Bonds of Christian Freedom*. London: Banner of Truth, 1645.
Booth, Abraham. *The Reign of Grace*. Grand Rapids: Eerdmans, 1949.
Buchanan, James. *The Doctrine of Justification*. London: Banner of Truth, 1961.
Ryle, J. C. *Holiness*. London: James Clarke, 1956.
Ryrie, Charles C. *The Grace of God*. Chicago: Moody, 1963.
———. *Balancing the Christian Life*. Chicago: Moody, 1969.
Shank, Robert. *Life in the Son*. Springfield, Mo.: Westcott Pub., 1960.
Stott, John R. *Confess Your Sins*. Philadelphia: Westminster, 1964.
Warfield, B. B. *The Plan of Salvation*. Grand Rapids: Eerdmans, 1942.
———. *Perfectionism*. Grand Rapids: Baker, 1958.
Whale, J. S. *Victor and Victim*. London: Cambridge U. Press, 1960.